Football Now!

MIKE RYAN

Fourth Edition

Football Now!

FIREFLY BOOKS

A FIREFLY BOOK

For Ollie Muirhead, the toughest little man I've ever known

Published by Firefly Books Ltd. 2015

First printing

Publisher Cataloging-in-Publication Data (U.S.)
Ryan, Mike, 1974-
     Football now! : today's gridiron greats / Mike Ryan.
4th edition
[160] pages : color photographs ; cm.
Includes index.
Summary: "The book celebrates more than 65 of the best current National Football League players, and the author has chosen the best players from each position on both sides of the ball" – Provided by publisher.
ISBN-13: 978-1-77085-282-2 (pbk.)
1. National Football League – Biography. 2. National Football League – Pictorial works. 3. Football players – United States – Biography.
I. Title.
796.332/0922 dc23   GV939.A1R935 2015

Library and Archives Canada Cataloguing in Publication
Ryan, Mike, 1974-, author
     Football now! : today's gridiron greats / Mike Ryan. -- Fourth edition.
Includes index.
First-Second editions by Mike Leonetti and John Iaboni.
ISBN 978-1-77085-282-2 (paperback)
1. Football players--United States--Biography. 2. National Football League. 3. National Football League--Pictorial works. 4. Football players--
United States--Pictorial works. I. Title.
GV939.A1R93 2015   796.332092'2
C2015-905124-X

Published in the United States by
Firefly Books (U.S.) Inc.
P.O. Box 1338, Ellicott Station
Buffalo, New York 14205

Published in Canada in 2015 by
Firefly Books Ltd.
50 Staples Avenue, Unit 1
Richmond Hill, Ontario L4B 0A7

Cover and interior design: Luna Design

Printed in Canada

The publisher gratefully acknowledges the financial support for our publishing program by the Government of Canada through the Canada Book Fund as administered by the Department of Canadian Heritage.

Photo Credits
Icon Sportswire

Hector Acevedo 19, 66
Justin Berl 41
Mark Bloom 74
Zach Bolinger 52, 53, 55, 75, 76, 77, 84, 90, 92, 93, 96, 130
Jeffrey Brown 95
Matt Cohen 17
Justin Cooper 134
Jim Dedmon 8, 22, 23, 61, 65, 100, 124
Frank DiBrango 103
Andrew Dieb 83, 109
Nuccio Dinuzzo 60
David Eulitt 21
Rich Gabrielson 20, 64, 131
Daniel Gluskoter 45, 67, 80, 117, 151

Al Golub 16
Rich Graessle 57, 148
Scott Grau 136
Patrick Green 6, 30
John Hefti 114, 121
Dennis Hubbard 69, 72, 73
Leslie Plaza Johnson 143
Rich Kane 8, 29, 32, 33, 34, 38, 39, 42, 54, 71, 106, 107, 126, 147, 152, 153
Todd Kirkland 85, 88, 125, 154
John Korduner 104
Daniel Kucin Jr. 94
Kenneth K. Lam 14, 15
Jeff Lewis 49, 116
Richard Lewis 37, 63, 139, 158
Mark LoMoglio 62, 81, 91
Mark Lyons 36, 51
Rodger Mallison 82

Greg McWilliams 31
Nhat V. Meyer 48
Kellen Micah 11, 86, 99, 102, 110, 132, 144, 145, 149
Jeff Moffett 108
MSA 12, 78, 127, 138, 160
Doug Murray 112, 137
Albert Pena 43
William Purnell 122, 139
Orlando Ramirez 5, 24, 25, 47, 68, 79, 97
Sam Riche 135
John Rivera 111, 113, 142
Juan Salas 10, 27, 59, 87, 138
John Sommers 40
Ric Tapia 2-3, 46, 101, 120, 156, 157
Scott Terna 70
TMB 18
Tom Walko 159

Joshua Weisberg 155
Cliff Welch 13, 26, 28, 50, 98, 105, 114, 128, 129, 146, 150
Bruce Yeung 44
Baltimore Sun/Zumapress 119
Contra Costa Times/Zumapress 35
Vinny Carchietta/Zumapress 58, 89
Kansas City Star/Zumapress 123
Zumapress 56, 118, 133

Cover:
Daniel Gluskoter (Rodgers)
Hector Acevedo (Wilson)
John Rivera (Watt)

Back Cover:
Albert Pena (Bryant)
Cliff Welch (Peterson)

Contents

Introduction

When I wrote the last edition of *Football Now!*, the NFL was coming off a lockout. In the face of a worldwide recession, the optics were bad, but those issues seem almost quaint now.

More recently the NFL has dealt with a lawsuit by former players about concussion-related brain injuries, the suicides of former players, and the ugly stain of domestic violence and the league office concealing what it knew about the violence and when.

Yet the NFL doesn't just endure; it thrives.

The regular season pregame show was the third-most popular program in the country last year, behind *Sunday Night Football* and *The Big Bang Theory*. The NFL accounted for nine of the top-10 most watched sporting events in 2014, with only the opening ceremony of the Olympics slipping in at number nine. The Super Bowl breaks its own record for viewership each year, and XLIX had the most viewers of any show in American TV history, with 72 percent of all TVs in the country tuned to the game.

It helped that Super Bowl XLIX had one of the most thrilling finishes ever. But that triumph, for the Patriots and the league, was punctured after Tom Brady was suspended and the team fined and docked draft picks for playing with underinflated balls. Compared to problems faced by the league earlier, however, and by those living in the real world, it was a tempest in a T-formation, but it's the kind of soap opera story line that keeps fans hooked. America loves a fall from grace almost as much as a story of redemption, and the game has its heroes and villains, drama and heartbreak, ferocity, passion and balletic grace.

Football also strengthens community and family bonds, and gives young players confidence and a sense of belonging, and the men they look up to can be a positive force for change. After Michael Brown was shot by a police officer, five St. Louis Rams showed their solidarity with thousands of protesters in Ferguson, Missouri, when they took to the field with the hands-up gesture. Theirs was a bigger stage — arguably the biggest in the country — and they used it as a platform for social justice.

Cleveland Browns wide receiver Andrew Hawkins joined them by wearing a shirt in support of 12-year-old Tamir Rice and John Crawford III, both killed by police, and being widely condemned for it.

"I was taught that justice is a right that every American should have," said Hawkins. "Also, justice should be the goal of every American. I think that's what makes this country. To me, justice means the innocent should be found innocent. It means that those who do wrong should get their due punishment. Ultimately, it means fair treatment. So a call for justice shouldn't offend or disrespect anybody. A call for justice shouldn't warrant an apology."

It was a powerful statement, and it went against the common belief that NFL players are motivated by self-interest and are willfully ignorant of the world, or inarticulate and uninformed.

And consider the words of player Michael Sam, written one year after publicly coming out as a gay man and being overwhelmingly supported by teammates and players around the NFL: "Football has always been a constant, positive force in my life, and many of the greatest experiences of my life have come from the game. Football has been there for me at times when few others have. It's pure and it's good, and it's what I do. I love football."

Hawkins and Sam aren't in this book, but the ones who made the cut are also fascinating, nuanced characters. They're some of the world's best athletes, but each has had to sacrifice and fight to get to the top of the game, overcoming hardship, loss, doubt and fear.

I hope you enjoy reading about them as much as I did when getting to know them. They're the reason football remains the most popular sport in America.

QUARTERBACKS

NEW ENGLAND PATRIOTS
★ ★ ★
QUARTERBACK
12

TOM BRADY

After Super Bowl XLIX, the cover of *Sports Illustrated* read, "On to Immortality," with an action shot of the man who won his fourth title and third Super Bowl MVP award. It might have had one extra letter and perhaps should have stated, "Immorality."

Tom Brady grew up in San Mateo, California, as a fan of the San Francisco 49ers and legendary quarterback Joe Montana. That Brady is chasing Montana for title of best big-game quarterback in NFL history is something no one saw coming.

Soft-spoken like Montana,

Brady has an inner fire that was stoked while he played at the University of Michigan. Considered skinny and slow, he focused on winning over his teammates instead of fans, and he learned to use slights as motivation.

Given more fuel as he waited until the sixth round to be drafted in 2000 by the New England Patriots — 199th overall — Brady took the league by storm. By the end of the 2001–02 season, he was New England's starting quarterback, a Super Bowl champion and a Super Bowl MVP. He followed

that up with Super Bowl titles after the 2003 and 2004 seasons, with his second MVP in Super Bowl XXXVIII (2003).

In 2007 it looked as if the Patriots were on their way to their fourth Super Bowl of the decade after Brady set an NFL single-season record with 50 touchdowns, won his first regular season MVP award and led the team to a 16-0 regular-season record. But a funny thing happened on the way to perfection. Behind Eli Manning and one of the most unlikely and amazing catches in NFL history, the New York Giants upset the Patriots to win Super Bowl XLII 17–14.

In the first game of the 2008 season, Brady suffered a devastating knee injury that cost him a year of football. But he came back strong, and in 2010 he became the first player in NFL history to be unanimously selected as league MVP. In 2011 the Patriots made it back to the Super Bowl in a highly anticipated rematch with the Giants. It was a chance for revenge and a 17th postseason win that would break his tie with Montana. With the ball in his hand and just under a minute left, Brady drove New England down the field, but his Hail Mary

pass on the final play was batted down, and the Giants won Super Bowl XLVI 21–17.

Brady broke Montana's postseason record for wins the following season, but by 2014 it looked as though the best years of his career were behind him. After a poor start, pundits were suggesting Brady retire with some dignity intact. He responded by leading New England to a 12-4 record, compiling one of his best statistical seasons.

IN THE HUDDLE

Brady has the most playoff starts (29) and wins (21) of any quarterback in NFL history, and holds the all-time postseason and Super Bowl records for passing yards, completions and touchdowns.

At 37 and in his 15th season, Brady turned back the clock in Super Bowl XLIX, winning his first title in a decade. It was a 28–24 come-from-behind squeaker that needed a New England goal-line stop to beat the Seattle Seahawks. Brady set a Super Bowl record with 37 completions, and he tied Montana with his fourth title and third Super Bowl MVP award.

It should have been a tidy storybook ending to a season. But leading up to the Super Bowl, the media focus was on "Deflategate." Brady was accused of colluding with locker-room attendants to have the air pressure in the balls lower than the rulebook-mandated 12.5 psi. The rule-breaking balls were discovered during the AFC Championship Game and were replaced in the second half by officials. Statistically the balls hardly made a difference in the Patriots' 45-7 win over the Indianapolis Colts.

The team brushed it off and

won one of the most thrilling Super Bowls in history. But in May 2015 the 243-page Wells Report was released, in which lawyer Ted Wells concluded that "it was more probable than not" that Brady was "at least generally aware" that the balls had been deflated. In the fuzzy logic of the NFL, that was enough to convict Brady and the Patriots. He was suspended for the first four games of the 2015 season, and the team was fined $1 million and lost two draft picks. It appears that Commissioner Roger Goodell bases his punishments more on the court of public opinion than on any legal or league precedents.

History will be the true judge of Brady, and whether Deflategate is seen as a minor indiscretion by a player obsessed

CAREER HIGHLIGHTS

- Two-time NFL MVP (2007, 2010)
- Three-time Super Bowl MVP (XXXVI, XXXVIII, XLIX)
- Ten-time Pro Bowl selection (2001, 2004–05, 2007, 2009–14)
- Two-time First Team All-Pro selection (2007, 2010)
- Second Team All-Pro (2005)
- 2009 Comeback Player of the Year
- Named to the NFL 2000s All-Decade Team

with winning is yet to be seen. He wasn't arrested and didn't use performance-enhancing drugs, but he allegedly tricked the American public, and that might be the biggest sin of them all.

DREW BREES

NEW ORLEANS SAINTS
★ ★ ★
QUARTERBACK
9

The man and the city needed each other. Both were battered and bruised, with a future that looked bleak. But America, built on tales of redemption, loves a second act.

On the final day of 2005, San Diego Chargers quarterback Drew Brees suffered a torn labrum and rotator cuff in his throwing shoulder. He underwent successful surgery, but his football future was in jeopardy. With Chargers quarterback-of-the-future Philip Rivers waiting in the wings, Brees' fate was sealed, and he was released from the team.

Earlier that year the city of New Orleans had been devastated by Hurricane Katrina. The city was in shambles, the confirmed death toll was close to 2,000 and the Superdome, home of the Saints, became a symbol of the city's darkest hour when people huddled there through the storm.

In the aftermath, the Saints played the majority of their home games at Louisiana State University in Baton Rouge and at the Alamodome in San Antonio, Texas, and the club struggled to a 3-13 record. The offseason, however, brought the quarterback and the city together. "It was a calling," said Brees. "[My wife and I] were brought here for a reason."

At a time when New Orleans felt abandoned by the country, Brees and his wife Brittany embraced the city, rebuilding an old home in the north end and becoming visibly active in the community. After arriving, they set up the Brees Dream Foundation to help fight cancer and provide "care, education and opportunities for children in need," which includes building downtown playgrounds and repairing football fields.

"He symbolizes the people of New Orleans in many, many ways," says NFL Commissioner Roger Goodell. "Drew believes in that community. He believes in doing what's right. He's one of the most genuine people I've ever met."

IN THE HUDDLE

Brees holds NFL records with nine consecutive seasons of at least 4,000 yards passing and four seasons of 5,000-plus, and his streak of 54 straight games with a touchdown pass broke a record that stood since 1960. He's also the most accurate passer in NFL history (66.2 percent).

Brees is also a leader on the field. After joining a team that had been mired in mediocrity for many years, he led the Saints in his first season all the way to the NFC Championship, which they lost to the Chicago Bears.

The city finally had something to rally around. The culmination of civic pride came on February 7, 2010, when Brees tied a championship record with 32 completions and took home the MVP award, as the Saints beat the Indianapolis Colts 31–17 in Super Bowl XLIV. It was the franchise's first championship, and it set off one of the biggest parties in the history of a town known for its revelry.

Brees followed that up with one of the most prolific seasons in NFL history in 2011. He won the Offensive Player of the Year award after breaking Dan Marino's 27-year-old single-season record for passing yards, which he did with a

CAREER HIGHLIGHTS

- First Team All-Pro (2006)
- Three-time Second Team All-Pro selection (2008, 2009, 2011)
- Nine-time Pro Bowl selection (2004, 2006, 2008–09, 2010–14)
- Two-time Offensive Player of the Year (2008, 2011)
- Super Bowl XLIV MVP (2010)
- Walter Payton Man of the Year (2006)
- NFL Comeback Player of the Year (2004)

game to spare, finishing the season with 5,476 yards. Brees also set records for completions in a season (468) and completion percentage (71.2 percent), while throwing 46 touchdowns.

The Saints won the division title with a 13-3 record, and in the playoffs Brees threw for over 460 yards in each game they played, with seven touchdowns and a quarterback rating of 110.1. But they lost to the San Francisco 49ers in the divisional playoff. "Bountygate" — the scandal in which coaches paid defensive players to injure opponents — derailed the Saints' momentum afterwards, and the resulting suspensions ruined the 2012 season for the Saints.

Back to relative normalcy in 2013, the Saints had an 11-5 record, and Brees had a third straight 5,000-yard season. In 2014 he had 456 completions for 4,952 yards, 33 touchdowns and a 97.0 passer rating. He ranked first in the league in completions and attempts, tied for first in passing yards and was second in completion percentage. The Saints, however, missed the playoffs at 7-9,

and in a measure of the incredibly high standards he's set, 2014 was considered a down year for the quarterback.

Since arriving in the Big Easy in 2006, Brees has missed only one game and leads the NFL with 43,685 passing yards, 5,649 attempts, 3,812 completions and 316 touchdowns passes, all franchise records.

He can't play forever though, and the Saints know that. Leading up to Brees' fifteenth season in the NFL and tenth in New Orleans, the franchise drafted quarterback Garrett Grayson of Colorado State in the third round of the 2015 draft. "I have no problem sitting behind a Hall of Famer like Drew Brees and learning," said the newest Saint.

For Brees, building up Grayson will be just another brick in the legacy he's constructing in his adopted hometown.

JOE FLACCO

Maybe it's because he came from a lower-division college, or because he's not married to a supermodel or hasn't hosted *Saturday Night Live*, but Joe Flacco doesn't get much respect when the conversation turns to the NFL's best quarterbacks. It matters little to the Baltimore Ravens and their fans, however, because he's steady and reliable, and he shines when he's needed most.

At Audubon High School in New Jersey, Flacco posted the fourth-highest career yardage total in South Jersey history. Stuck on the sidelines at the University of Pittsburgh, Flacco transferred to the University of Delaware. In two seasons as a Blue Hen, he set 20 school records, including career completions (595) and passing yards per game (284.2).

That was good enough for

His stoicism comes from a lesson his father, Steve, taught him at an early age. "My dad's my best friend," explains Flacco. "The biggest thing he preached was being tough. I think a tough guy doesn't really show many emotions. Not to say that I don't have emotion… But when things are going bad, as a leader, you can't act like anything is wrong. You go out there and take each snap like it's the same, no matter what the score is, no matter what happened on the last play."

IN THE HUDDLE

In a 2014 win over the Tampa Bay Buccaneers, Flacco became the fastest player in NFL history to throw five touchdown passes, doing it in the first 16:03.

the Baltimore Ravens to take the 6-foot-6, 245-pound quarterback 18th overall in 2008.

Flacco started from day one in Baltimore and hasn't missed a game since. He took the Ravens to the AFC Championship Game in his rookie year, losing to the Pittsburgh Steelers, and he racked up 44 regular-season wins from 2008 through 2011, the most by a quarterback in his first four years in NFL history.

In the 2011 playoffs, the Ravens came within a dropped pass of beating the New England Patriots to reach the Super Bowl, but in the offseason a SportsNation online poll revealed that 61 percent of 95,000 respondents indicated Flacco was not an "elite" quarterback. He proved them wrong in 2012 when he beat superstars Peyton Manning and Tom Brady on the road to Super Bowl XLVII, where he was named MVP after throwing for three touchdowns in a 34–31 victory over the San Francisco 49ers.

Flacco had 1,140 yards passing and 11 touchdowns during the playoff run joining Joe Montana and Kurt Warner for the most touchdown passes in a single postseason. He tied Tom Brady for the most playoff victories in a quarterback's first five seasons, with nine, and he's the only quarterback since the 1970 merger to win a playoff game in each of his first five seasons.

"Will people finally buy how good this guy is?" asked coach John Harbaugh during the playoff run.

In 2014, Flacco set career highs in passing yards (3,986) and touchdown passes (27), while the Ravens set franchise single-season records in yards (5,838) and points scored (409).

In the 2014 playoffs, Baltimore beat the archrival Steelers before losing 35–31 to the eventual champion Patriots. Flacco completed 46 of 74 passes (62.2 percent) for 551 yards and six touchdowns, including a single-game team record for the playoffs with four touchdown passes against the Patriots.

Flacco's ten career playoff victories since 2008 are three more than Brady, who is next on the list, and his seven career road wins in the playoffs are the most by any quarterback in NFL history. He also set an NFL record by throwing at least two touchdowns in eight straight playoff games.

Saying Flacco's a playoff quarterback shortchanges him though, as he's also posted three of the top-4 passing games and five of the top-6 passing seasons in team history. He owns the career franchise marks for passing yards, touchdowns and completions, and his 72 career regular-season wins since 2008 are just two behind Brady and Manning, who are tied for first.

So maybe it's time to rethink the quarterback hierarchy. Flacco is unflappable when the pressure is highest, and his regular-season stats are consistently excellent.

But the unassuming and stoic star probably doesn't care. As long as his teammates respect him and

he can return to his wife, Dana, and sons, Stephen and Daniel, at their home after games (a mile from his parents' house), he's fine. And some opinions matter more than the media's.

"He seems like he's very kind to everyone that he comes in contact with," says Special Olympian Daniel Hays, whom Flacco spent time with through Special Olympics Maryland. "When I look around at my fellow athletes seeing that Joe and the Ravens take their time out to help show us the skills in football… it shows that they think of people with intellectual disabilities as athletes out on the field. It really means a lot that they see past those barriers."

CAREER HIGHLIGHTS

- Super Bowl XLVII MVP
- Two-time USA TODAY All-Joe Team (2009, 2012)
- 82 total wins (including playoffs) are the most by a quarterback since 2008, when he entered the league
- 72 regular-season victories are the most by a quarterback in the first seven seasons of a career (2008–14)
- Ravens' all-time leader in passing yards (25,531), touchdown passes (148), completions (2,213) and attempts (3,657)

COLIN KAEPERNICK

When Colin Kaepernick was in fourth grade, he wrote himself a letter about his future. The letter says, "I hope I go to a good college in football and then go to the pros and play on the Niners or the Packers, even if they're not good in seven years."

Born in Milwaukee in 1987, Kaepernick was given up for adoption as an infant by his mother, Heidi Russo. Adoptive parents Rick and Teresa Kaepernick, who had two children, Kyle and Devon, had also lost two infants to heart defects.

"We stopped," said Teresa of trying to have a bigger family. "But after about five years, I had a very strong desire to have another child. God works in mysterious ways, because I just had such an overwhelming urge at that time. We were so lucky to get Colin."

The Kaepernicks moved to California, where Colin excelled in sports. At John H. Pitman High School in Turlock, Kaepernick was an All-State nominee in football, basketball and baseball. He threw two no-hitters in his senior season and was drafted by MLB's Chicago Cubs in 2009, but he chose to pursue his childhood football dream instead.

Despite being All-District, All-Conference and All-Academic in high school, the major colleges were put off by his awkward throwing motion and scrawny frame. So he went to a tryout at the University of Nevada and was offered a scholarship as a safety. In the fifth game of his freshman year, he took over as quarterback when the starter was injured, and he never came out. In his first full game, he accounted for 420 yards in a 69–67 overtime loss to 25-point favorites Boise State.

Over four seasons with the Wolf Pack, Kaepernick threw for

10,098 yards and 82 touchdowns, while rushing for 4,112 yards and 59 touchdowns. He became the only quarterback in NCAA history to run for over 1,000 yards in three consecutive seasons and to have over 10,000 yards passing and 4,000 rushing. Yet he lasted until the second round of the 2011 draft.

His early letter proved prescient, as the San Francisco 49ers traded up nine spots to pick Kaepernick 36th overall. He spent his rookie year backing up Alex Smith, but took over in Week 11 of the 2012 season when Smith suffered a concussion.

Smith had almost led the 49ers to the Super Bowl in 2011 and was among the league leaders in quarterback rating when he was hurt, so a few eyebrows were raised when Jim Harbaugh named Kaepernick as the permanent number one. It had been earned, however, with five wins in his first seven starts.

IN THE HUDDLE

After six playoff games, Kaepernick is second in NFL history among quarterbacks with 507 career postseason rushing yards, behind former 49er Steve Young, who had 594 yards in 20 career playoff games. Kaepernick also has three of the top-5 single-game rushing totals by a quarterback in the postseason.

In Kaepernick's first playoff appearance, he set a single-game rushing record for quarterbacks (both in regular season and postseason), with 181 yards, and outplayed superstar Aaron Rodgers in a win over the heavily favored Green Bay Packers, his parents' favorite team. After squeaking by the Atlanta Falcons in the conference championship, he made his tenth career start at Super Bowl XLVII. Down 28–6 to the Baltimore Ravens when a power outage caused a lengthy delay, Kaepernick led a furious comeback, but the 49ers fell short on their final drive and lost 34–31.

In the 2013 season, he ran for 524 yards, the second most by a quarterback in franchise history, and

he was the first San Francisco quarterback to throw 20 touchdowns in 11 years. The 49ers had a 12-4 record, and Kaepernick became the fourth quarterback in NFL history to win his first three career playoff games on the road, after again beating the Packers as well as the Carolina Panthers. The 49ers, however, lost to the eventual champion Seattle Seahawks in the NFC title game.

With high expectations for another deep playoff run, the 49ers were beset by injuries and scandal in 2014 and slid back among the pack with an 8-8 record. They missed the playoffs and Harbaugh lost his job. Kaepernick, however, had career highs in passing yards (3,369) and rushing yards (639), and in a game against the San Diego Chargers, his 90-yard run became the second longest by a quarterback in NFL history and by anyone in a 49er uniform. Kaepernick finished the game with 151 yards, and running back Frank Gore had 158, making them the fourth teammates in history to both go over 150 yards in a game, and the first since 1976.

Kaepernick has strong religious beliefs — displayed in his myriad tattoos — which

he'll call upon in 2015 as the new leader of the team. With several veterans retiring, the fate of the 49ers rests on his shoulders, and new and enthusiastic coach Jim Tomsula has faith that he'll come through. "He's a great dude… Colin's a great football player and even better person. We're really excited about Colin."

Kaepernick is excited too. He worked on his throwing motion in the off-season and even created a personal hashtag (#7tormsComing) to highlight his preparation for the 2015 season. He did make one blunder when he used his hashtag in conjunction with the deadly floods in Houston. He quickly took down the tweet and apologized.

His early success may have obscured the fact that he's still young, and he's still learning.

CAREER HIGHLIGHTS

- Two-time USA Today All-Joe Team (2012–13)
- Holds the single-game quarterback rushing record for the regular season or postseason, with 181 yards
- Two-time WAC Offensive Player of the Year (2010, 2012)

ANDREW LUCK

It's been done before, but it's rare and it's difficult. As Steve Young followed Joe Montana in San Francisco and Aaron Rodgers took over for Brett Favre in Green Bay, Andrew Luck was tasked with making people in Indianapolis forget that Peyton Manning, arguably the best quarterback in NFL history, was gone.

Luck might've been set up to handle such pressure from an early age, with his unusual path and unique perspective. His father, Oliver, was a Houston Oilers quarterback and the general manager of two World League of American Football teams, which meant young Andrew lived in London and Frankfurt before the family settled back in Houston.

At Stratford High in Houston, Luck threw for 7,139 yards and 53 touchdowns and had 2,085 yards rushing. The 2008 co-valedictorian chose Stanford University, spurning scholarship offers from schools with major football programs for an academic institution with a team that went 1-11 the year before he enrolled.

Success traveled from Stratford to Stanford, where Luck had a 3.48 GPA as an architectural design major and won 31 of the 38 games he played — the most wins by a Cardinal quarterback and the highest winning percentage in school history. He was a Heisman Trophy finalist in 2010 and 2011 and set school records for completion percentage (67.0),

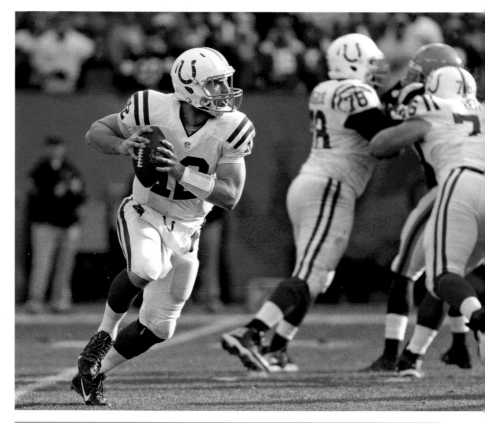

CAREER HIGHLIGHTS

- Three-time Pro Bowl selection (2012–14)
- Led the NFL in touchdown passes in 2014 (40)
- Set the franchise record with yards passing in 2014 (4,761)
- Holds the NFL record for the most passing yards in a player's first five postseason games (1,703)
- Holds NFL rookie records for passing yards in a game (433) and season (4,374)
- Winner of the Maxwell Award for National Collegiate Player of the Year and the Walter Camp Football Foundation Player of the Year (2011)

touchdown passes (82) and rushing yards by a quarterback (957).

At Stanford, Luck had a kindred spirit and mentor in coach Jim Harbaugh, the former NFL quarterback. (Harbaugh since coached the San Francisco 49ers to a Super Bowl appearance before returning to the college ranks with the University of Michigan.) Stanford, with Harbaugh, was the best possible schooling for a future in the NFL, and though many thought Luck was NFL-ready after his junior year, he returned to complete his degree. He ran the risk of hurting himself or his draft prospects, but he won the Maxwell Award as the nation's top player, the Walter Camp Football Foundation Player of the Year award and the Johnny Unitas Golden Arm Award.

IN THE HUDDLE

In 2014, Luck became the first player in NFL history with at least 350 passing yards in five consecutive road games, and he's the first to post consecutive games with at least 370 passing yards, four or more touchdown passes, a completion percentage above 70 and one or no interceptions.

Meanwhile in Indianapolis, the Colts — without Manning — were lurching to an NFL-worst 2-14 season in 2011. After several neck surgeries and the possibility he'd be a shadow of his former self while taking up a large chunk of the salary cap, Manning was released before the 2012 season. The timing was impeccable.

In 2012 the Colts got Luck first overall and became the story of the season. Led by their precocious new quarterback and motivated by coach Chuck Pagano's battle with leukemia, the Colts went 11-5.

Playing in a very different system than at Stanford, Luck proved that he's a quick study. After some initial jitters, he absorbed the playbook and set an NFL rookie record with 4,374 yards passing and won more games as a rookie than any quarterback picked first overall in history. He also became

the first rookie to start a postseason game — a loss to the Baltimore Ravens.

Back in the playoffs after another 11-5 season in 2013, Luck led the Colts to a win against the Kansas City Chiefs after being down by 28 points in the third quarter, the second-biggest comeback in NFL history. That cemented Luck's place in Colts lore and won over the few remaining doubters.

Pagano is healthy and back on the sideline, and Luck now holds league records for the most yards in a quarterback's first two and three seasons (8,196 and 12,957, respectively). He also joined Manning and Hall of Famer Dan Marino as the only players to pass for 4,000 yards in two of their first three NFL seasons.

In 2014, Luck broke Manning's franchise record with 4,761 yards, and he was tops in the league with 40 touchdown passes, one more than Manning. In a script that the NFL would've written if it could, the two met in the second round

of the playoffs, with Luck getting the better of his predecessor in a 24–13 win over the Broncos in Denver.

The comparisons are inevitable. Like Manning, Luck is one of the game's good guys, he plays an intelligent game that will help him thrive when the physical gifts begin to fade, and he's wise enough to keep away from off-field drama. While he calls himself "tremendously honored" to be mentioned in the same conversation as Manning, Luck is also careful to separate himself.

"Peyton set the bar for being a quarterback, and certainly for being a quarterback in this town. But I do not live in Peyton Manning's world. I feel like the media has made me out to be more like him than I really am."

The Colts know how lucky they are to have two of the greats in back-to-back generations, and Luck gives them the luxury of focusing on the present, not on past glories.

"One of the good things about being here is I don't feel I'm being held to some Peyton Manning standard. I'm just trying to be me," says Luck.

The Colts are just fine with that.

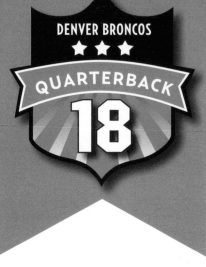

DENVER BRONCOS
★ ★ ★

QUARTERBACK

18

PEYTON MANNING

When the Indianapolis Colts released Peyton Manning in the spring of 2012, he could have easily retired. He would have gone down as one of the best players — and men — in NFL history and as a certain first-ballot Hall of Famer. But he didn't retire. He risked permanent injury and the possibility that he'd end his career with a whimper, because he wanted another Super Bowl. He didn't come back to appease the critics who've claimed that his winning only one championship diminished his legacy; he came back because the competitive fires still burned brightly.

Manning didn't play a down during the 2011 season, but his shadow loomed large. The Colts went from a perennial contender to last in the league. Spinal fusion surgery in his neck put an end to Manning's 277 straight games, and his release by the Colts ushered in the Andrew Luck era in Indianapolis and ended one of the NFL's most successful marriages. Courted by much of the league and signed by the Denver Broncos, Manning continues to bark *Omaha* at the line of scrimmage, and to add to his records and stature.

Manning's run on the NFL record books started in 1998. Indianapolis, with their rookie quarterback, managed to win just three games, but Manning set five NFL rookie records, including most touchdown passes (26). The following season the Colts set an NFL record with a 10-win turnaround to finish 13-3, winning 11 of their final 12 games, with Manning throwing for 4,135 yards. It just got better from there.

IN THE HUDDLE
In 2013, Manning set NFL single-season records for passing yards (5,477), yards per game (342.3), touchdowns (55), four-touchdown games (9) and two-touchdown games (15), and the Broncos had the most points (606) and touchdowns (76) in NFL history.

Manning earned NFL MVP honors in 2003, 2004, 2008 and 2009, while becoming the Colts' all-time leader in career wins (141), passing yards (54,828), pass attempts (7,210), pass completions (4,682) and passing touchdowns (399). His finest hour came on February 4, 2007, when he led Indianapolis to a 29–17 victory over the Chicago Bears in Super Bowl XLI and was named the game's MVP. He

CAREER HIGHLIGHTS

- Five-time NFL MVP (2003–04, 2008–09, 2013)
- Super Bowl XLI MVP
- Fourteen-time Pro Bowl selection (1999–2000, 2002–10, 2012–14)
- Seven-time First Team All-Pro selection (2003–05, 2008–09, 2012–13)
- Three-time Second Team All-Pro selection (1999–2000, 2006)
- 2012 Comeback Player of the Year
- Named to NFL 2000s All-Decade Team
- Holds the NFL record for career touchdown passes (530)

brought the Colts back to the big dance three years later, but the New Orleans Saints prevailed 31–17 in Super Bowl XLIV.

When it came time for Manning to leave the Colts, the quarterback conducted himself with the same class he always had. Manning stood alongside Colts owner Jim Irsay and he emotionally thanked the city and organization, saying goodbye to the only professional home he'd ever known.

Concerns over his ability to return after major surgery and a full year off from football were quickly dispelled in the 2012 season. Manning transformed the previously 8-8 Broncos to 13-3 winners and was named Comeback Player of the Year. In 2013 he had the most offensively impressive season of his career. Denver opened the campaign against the defending champion Baltimore Ravens, and Manning threw a record-tying seven touchdown passes on his way to setting the single-season NFL records for touchdowns passes

(55) and passing yards (5,477). He also won an unprecedented fifth MVP award, two more than anyone in NFL history.

After blowing through the playoffs, the NFL talking heads were ready to anoint Manning as the greatest of all time. All he had to do was beat the Seattle Seahawks in Super Bowl XLVIII. The first snap of the game went over Manning's head and into the end zone for a Seattle safety, and it went downhill from there. The final score was 43–8 for the Seahawks, and the knives came out to cut Manning down to size.

In 2014, Manning surpassed Brett Favre for most touchdown passes in NFL history (530 and counting) and threw for over 4,000 yards for a record 14th season. He was second in the league with 39 touchdown passes, one fewer than Luck, who also bested of him in the playoffs as the Colts beat the Broncos 24–13 in the divisional round.

Manning is a virtual lock to pass Favre for the all-time records in career completions

and yards, but he's still seeking his second Super Bowl.

If Manning needs any more motivation, Tom Brady, his competition for the best quarterback of all time, won his fourth Super Bowl title after the 2014 season. In the aftermath some air has been let out of Brady's reputation, but there's never been any hint of cheating in Manning's career.

Manning has won numerous humanitarian awards, is a favorite pitchman for corporate America and has hosted *Saturday Night Live*. He's so admired that his name has spiked in popularity in each of the states he's played in. When he was named *Sports Illustrated's* Sportsman of the Year after his historic 2013 season, the magazine chronicled several of the people named after him.

As Kim Dukes says of her son Peyton, "We raised him to be a good, honest person, and that's the most important thing he shares with his namesake."

CAROLINA PANTHERS
★ ★ ★
QUARTERBACK
1

CAM NEWTON

With sublime talent, supreme confidence, model good looks and a knack for making headlines, Cam Newton was born to shine. On the biggest stages and in small markets, he finds a way to stand out.

After graduating from Westlake High School in Atlanta, Georgia, Cam Newton had more than 40 scholarship offers. He chose the University of Florida because the Gators' offensive system suited his game, and he was confident he could unseat established star Tim Tebow and become the starting quarterback.

IN THE HUDDLE

Newton is the first player in NFL history to have 10,000 passing yards and 2,000 rushing yards in their first four seasons, and the first to have at least 3,000 passing yards and 500 rushing yards in four consecutive seasons.

Newton's career in Florida turned out to be pretty quiet — on the field at least. As a freshman in 2007, he played five games, threw for a total of 40 yards and ran for 103. In his first game as a sophomore, he injured his ankle and sat out the season as a medical redshirt. He was arrested for stealing a laptop that year, and though the charges were dropped after he agreed to a diversion program, the incident spelled the end of his time with Florida.

CAREER HIGHLIGHTS

- Two-time Pro Bowl selection (2011, 2013)

- NFL Offensive Rookie of the Year (2011)

- Holds the NFL record for single-season rushing touchdowns by a quarterback (14)

- Led the NFL with 5.6 yards per rushing attempt (2011)

- Heisman Trophy winner (2010)

In January 2009, Newton transferred to tiny Blinn College in Brenham, Texas, and he led the Buccaneers to the national junior college championship in his lone season there. This earned him the attention of the Division I schools for a second time. Spoiled again, he decided on Auburn University.

Newton had one of the best seasons in NCAA history, breaking a slew of school and conference records, winning every major individual trophy — including the Heisman — and leading Auburn to its first national title since 1957.

Newton had another year of eligibility, but with nothing left to prove or to win, he declared for the 2011 NFL draft. The Panthers snapped him up with the number one pick, and in his first game he threw for 422 yards, breaking Peyton Manning's record for an NFL debut. He followed that up with a 432-yard game, the most by a rookie quarterback in NFL history and the highest total after two career starts. Newton cruised from there, setting the record for rushing touchdowns by a quarterback, with 14, becoming the first rookie to have over 4,000 yards passing and going down in history as the first quarterback to ever have over 4,000 yards passing and 500 yards rushing in a season.

Any other year Newton probably would have been the biggest story in the league, but Tebow, starting for the Denver Broncos as a rookie, was stealing the spotlight with his fourth quarter comebacks and ascension to pop-culture fame.

While Tebow was a one-season wonder, Newton became a true star. He led the NFL in his second season with 13.8 yards per pass completion, and he's currently the career leader among active players, with 12.6. He's joined Randall Cunningham and Michael Vick as the only quarterbacks in NFL history with four or more seasons of at least 500 yards rushing, and his 33 rushing touchdowns are the most by a quarterback in their first four seasons. Astonishingly, only three running backs have more touchdowns than Newton since he entered the league in 2011.

The real measure of success for a quarterback, however, is in team leadership, and Newton led Carolina to become the NFC South's first ever back-to-back division champions.

At 6-foot-5 and 245 pounds, Newton is built to take hits, unless they're by a car. He sat out for just the second game of his career after hurting his back and breaking ribs in a December 2014 accident. Playing through the pain, he earned his first playoff victory a few weeks later, a 27–16 win over the Arizona Cardinals, before falling to the Seattle Seahawks in the divisional round.

But the Panthers have faith that Newton can lead the team to playoff relevance, and rewarded him with a five-year, $103.7 million contract before the 2015 season.

According to Newton, the best is yet to come. In an interview on a Charlotte TV station in the off-season, the interviewer said, "You have been called the NFL's greatest talent as well as the NFL's greatest unknown. Do you agree with that?"

"Absolutely not," responded Newton. "And I say this with the most humility, but I don't think [there has ever been a player who has come close to] who I'm trying to be. Nobody has the size, nobody has the speed, nobody has the arm strength and nobody has the intangibles that I've had."

Not only is he self-assured and rich, but as the new face of Drakkar Essence cologne, he smells good too.

SAN DIEGO CHARGERS
QUARTERBACK 17

PHILIP RIVERS

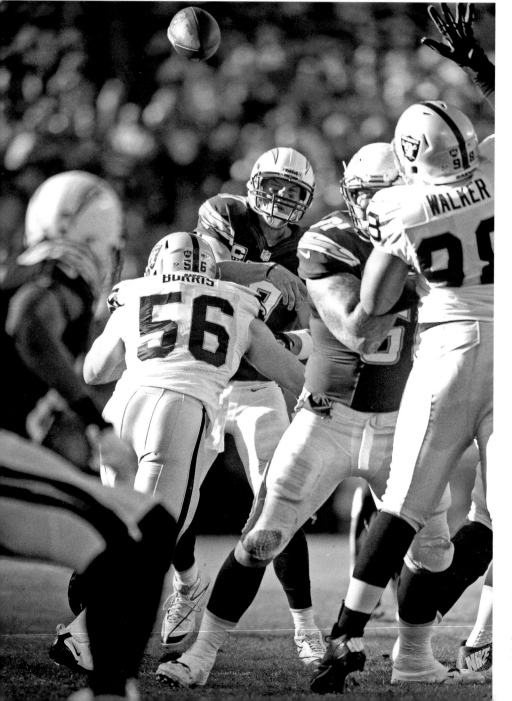

The San Diego Chargers' Philip Rivers is the Kevin Bacon of NFL quarterbacks: there are few degrees of separation between him and the league's other elite passers. Rivers was essentially swapped for Eli Manning on draft day when Manning refused to sign with San Diego, which had the first overall pick. Rivers was drafted fourth by the New York Giants in 2004, seven spots ahead of the Pittsburgh Steelers' Ben Roethlisberger, at 11. Once in San Diego, Rivers ended up wresting the starting job from Drew Brees, who's now breaking records with the New Orleans Saints.

Manning, Roethlisberger and Brees have all been named MVP in Super Bowl victories. Though Rivers ranks ahead of them in career passer rating, until he is able to join that exclusive club, he'll always come up short in ultimate quarterback comparisons.

Rivers has the tools to get there. He grew up with the game and was always poised and confident beyond his years. He was the starting quarterback and occasional free safety at Athens High in Alabama, where his dad coached, and he was voted the state's Player of the Year as a senior. He wasn't recruited as a quarterback by any marquee schools because of his unusual delivery. But North Carolina State University assistant coach Joe Pate had no reservations about Rivers' ability, saying, "I concentrated more on the results of his throws, and I realized he was the best quarterback that I'd ever recruited."

Rivers was the undisputed leader of the offense from his first season, earning the respect of his teammates and putting NC State on the football map for the first time in decades. The team had a winning record in each of his four seasons, ending three with a victory in a bowl game, and in his senior year he was named ACC Athlete of the Year and Senior Bowl MVP.

Despite his collegiate success and high draft spot, when Rivers reached the NFL he sat on the bench for two seasons. He didn't pout about it; he used that time to learn from veterans Brees and Doug Flutie. When he became the starter in 2006, the Chargers had enough confidence in Rivers to let Brees go.

IN THE HUDDLE

Rivers' career passer rating of 95.7 is sixth best all-time, ahead of Drew Brees and Ben Roethlisberger, who are seventh and eighth, respectively. He is 0.2 points behind Tom Brady.

In nine seasons since as a starter, Rivers has led the Chargers to four AFC West titles and four playoff wins, has thrown for over 4,000 yards seven times and hasn't missed a single game.

The 2012 season was Rivers' first under 4,000 yards, and the Chargers finished 7-9, his first losing season at any level. The following year he led the NFL with a 69.5 completion percentage and finished in the top 5 in yards per pass (8.23), passing yards (4,478), passing touchdowns (32) and quarterback rating (105.5). Although he hadn't gone anywhere, he won the 2013 Comeback Player of the Year award. In 2014 he was an early candidate for MVP after having a passer rating above 120 in five straight games, a first in league history. But postseason success

continues to elude him.

"Let me tell you right now, he's going to say the politically correct things because that's what you have to do as a player, but Philip Rivers is burning inside," says former teammate Lorenzo Neal. "Ben Roethlisberger has gone to three Super Bowls and won two. Eli Manning has gone to two Super Bowls and won both.

"I know Philip. He's a competitor. You see him on the field, how animated he is, how frustrated he gets. He wants to win a Super Bowl, trust me. This is his legacy."

If it's going to happen in San Diego, it will have to be soon. Antonio Gates, who shares the all-time quarterback-to-tight-end touchdown record with Rivers, is in the autumn of his career, and there's a possibility the franchise could move to Los Angeles.

If that's the case, Rivers could leave the team. The conservative Republican and devout Catholic has said he doesn't want to raise his seven children in Los Angeles, but Chargers general manager Tom

Telesco is committed to making him a career Charger.

"I've been crystal clear what our plans and intentions are. He's our quarterback, and hopefully for many, many years moving forward. I think he's got a lot of good years left in him. . . . Philip is our quarterback, and the plan is he's going to be here for a long, long, long time."

Telesco later told the *San Diego Union-Tribune*, "I don't like Philip as our QB; I love him. And I'll go to war with him."

AARON RODGERS

GREEN BAY PACKERS
★ ★ ★
QUARTERBACK
12

Many would crack under the pressure of being thrust into the spotlight when a legend is cast aside. Not Aaron Rodgers. With a preternatural calm, he went from unlikely to unparalleled.

At Pleasant Valley High School in Chico, California, Rodgers was a skinny senior with a rocket arm and size 14 feet,

who had just one college coach come to his house — by walking across the street. Neighbor Craig Rigsbee coached at Butte College, and in Rodgers' single season there he led the team to a 10-1 record. His talent caught the eye of Jeff Tedford, the head coach at the University of California, Berkeley, and Rodgers spent two seasons becoming the highest-rated passer in school history before declaring for the NFL draft a year early.

It's a good thing Rodgers has big feet, because he had big shoes to fill. The Green Bay Packers picked Rodgers 24th overall in 2005, in the midst of Brett Favre's reign. Favre had played every game for 16 seasons, won the MVP award three times and set NFL career records for completions, yards and touchdowns. So Rodgers threw all of 59 passes in his first three seasons. Choosing not to complain about the lack of playing time or opportunity, he focused on learning from his future Hall of Fame teammate.

The tables turned before the 2008 season, when Favre publicly flirted with other teams. The result was a messy divorce that ended with Rodgers taking the reins.

Ever the statesman, Rodgers

stayed away from the controversy and ushered in the new era in the best way possible in 2010. The Packers made the playoffs on the last day of the season and then beat each of the top-3 seeds in the NFC to reach Super Bowl XLV against the Pittsburgh Steelers. Rodgers became the fourth quarterback in history to throw for over 300 yards and 3 touchdowns in a Super Bowl, as he led the Packers to the title, earning the MVP award in the process.

IN THE HUDDLE
Rodgers made his 100th career start in 2014, and set NFL records for most passing yards (27,520), games without an interception (58), 100-plus passer rating games (60), best passer rating (107.3), and best touchdown-to-interception ratio (222-54) in a quarterback's first 100 games.

The Packers may not have repeated as champions in 2011, but in a year when Tom Brady and Drew Brees both surpassed Dan Marino's 27-year-old single-season passing record of 5,084 yards, the MVP award went to Rodgers. That season he set the single-season quarterback rating record of 122.5, upping his career rating to 104.1. He threw for

4,643 yards, with 45 touchdowns and only 6 interceptions. The Packers went 15-1.

Since then, Rodgers has burnished his legacy and Hall of Fame credentials. Limited to nine games in 2013 with a broken collarbone, he still set a new NFL record with his fifth straight season with a passer rating over 100, at 104.9. In 2014 he extended his record with his second-highest total, at 112.2. His career average of 106.0 is the best in NFL history, almost 10 points ahead of runner-up Tony Romo.

The Packers started the 2014 season with a 1-2 record. Fans, used to the team's high standards, pushed the panic button, theorizing that Rodgers' collarbone was still bothering him or that his relationship with actress Olivia Munn was a distraction.

After a loss to the Detroit Lions, when the Packers had the fewest yards of offense under Rodgers since 2008, the quarterback went on his weekly radio show to assure fans.

"Five letters here, just for everybody out there in Packerland. R-E-L-A-X. Relax. We're going to be okay." It put the pressure squarely on his shoulders and became the catchphrase of the season. The Packers proceeded to win 11 of their next 13 games and the NFC North title.

Hobbled by a torn calf muscle in the postseason, Rodgers led the Packers to a win over the Dallas Cowboys in the divisional round. In the NFC title game, the Packers coughed up a 12-point lead with just over two minutes left, losing to the defending champion Seattle Seahawks in overtime.

Days later, when Rodgers finally spoke about the game, he admitted that the loss would take awhile to recover from. "Every

CAREER HIGHLIGHTS

- Two-time NFL MVP (2011, 2014)
- Super Bowl XLV MVP
- Four-time Pro Bowl selection (2009, 2011–12, 2014)
- Two-time First Team All-Pro selection (2011, 2014)
- Second Team All-Pro (2012)
- Associated Press Male Athlete of the Year (2011)

year you get older in the league, your chances get fewer. That's why it stings a little bit more."

It wasn't the trophy he wanted, but two weeks later Rodgers was named MVP for the second time, taking 31 of 50 votes to beat out J.J. Watt, who had one of the most dominant seasons of any defender in history.

Rodgers, however, simply couldn't be ignored.

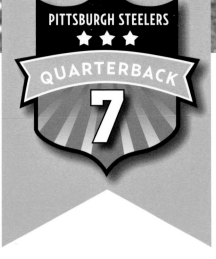

BEN ROETHLISBERGER

The 1983 draft is regarded as the deepest at quarterback in NFL history, with future Hall of Famers John Elway, Jim Kelly and Dan Marino all taken in the first round. The class of 2004 is giving these men a run for their money, thanks to the New York Giants' Eli Manning, the San Diego Chargers' Philip Rivers and the Pittsburgh Steelers' Ben Roethlisberger.

But it is Roethlisberger who's the head of the class.

The future All-Pro quarterback didn't even play the position at Ohio's Findlay High School until his senior year, when the coach's son graduated. In his one season at the helm, he set state records with 4,041 yards passing and 54 touchdowns, and won the Ohio Offensive Player of the Year award.

At Miami University (Ohio), Roethlisberger set 21 school records, including career completions (854), passing yards (10,829) and touchdown passes (84), and he was a three-time All-Mid-American Conference selection.

Roethlisberger left Miami after his junior year and was drafted 11th overall by the Steelers. He first saw NFL action in the second game of his rookie

season (2004), and he promptly won 13 straight games and set rookie records for wins, passer rating (98.1) and completion percentage (66.4).

After finishing 15-1 and getting as far as the AFC Championship in 2004, the Steelers had to rally in 2005 to win their last four games in order to reach the playoffs as a wild-card entry. Roethlisberger pulled it off and, playing through injury, led Pittsburgh to two playoff road

victories to reach the conference championship.

That AFC Championship Game on the road in Indianapolis looked bad for the Steelers when the Colts' Nick Harper picked up a fumble with less than two minutes left. Headed for what looked like a sure touchdown and a trip to the Super Bowl, Harper ran into the last man between him and the end zone — the 6-foot-4, 240-pound Roethlisberger, who brought Harper down with one arm and secured the win for Pittsburgh.

Roethlisberger's Super Bowl XL performance was equally memorable, but for the wrong reasons. He had one of the ugliest stat lines in history — 9 completions for 123 yards, no touchdowns and 2 interceptions — but the Steelers beat the Seattle Seahawks 21–10, which made Roethlisberger both the youngest quarterback and the lowest-rated passer to win the Super Bowl.

The Steelers reached the Super Bowl again in 2008, and far from being a nonfactor, Roethlisberger engineered the winning drive. Trailing 23–20 against the Arizona Cardinals and with just over two minutes left in the game, Roethlisberger took the Steelers 88 yards on eight plays, throwing an inch-perfect pass to Santonio Holmes in the corner of the end zone with 35 seconds left to win the game.

IN THE HUDDLE

In 2014, Roethlisberger set single-season team records with 4,952 passing yards, 408 completions, a 67.1 completion percentage, most 300-yard games (9), and games with a passer rating of 100-plus (10).

Roethlisberger's life, however, hasn't been quite as storybook. After a golf tournament in Lake Tahoe in 2008, a hotel employee accused him of sexual assault. The charges were eventually dropped, but Roethlisberger was arrested a second time in 2010 after an alleged encounter with a college student in Georgia. Prosecutors didn't pursue the case, but NFL Commissioner Roger Goodell suspended Roethlisberger for six games under the league's personal-conduct policy. Roethlisberger convinced Goodell he understood the gravity of his actions and was

going to turn his life around, so his suspension was later reduced to four games.

To his credit, Roethlisberger was named the Steelers' 2013 Walter Payton Man of the Year, an award that recognizes community service and playing excellence. His newfound maturity and deepened faith have translated to continued success on the field. Wife Ashley and children Baylee and Benjamin have also grounded him.

Big Ben, who owns virtually every passing record in Steelers history, became the fourth quarterback in NFL history (after Tom Brady, Joe Montana and former Steeler Terry Bradshaw) to win 100 games in the first 150 starts of his career, after defeating the Indianapolis Colts in Week 8 of 2014. Including that game and the one after it, he threw 12 touchdowns to set an NFL record for the most passing touchdowns in a two-game span, and in Week 10 he went over 3,000 yards passing for the ninth consecutive season — one of only six quarterbacks in NFL history to do so. At the end of the season he had set career and franchise highs in completions and completion percentage, and tied the New Orleans Saints' Drew Brees for the NFL lead with 4,952 passing yards, also a new Steelers record.

If Roethlisberger doesn't occupy the same penthouse of NFL stardom as the likes of Brady, Brees and Peyton Manning, he's in a sunken living room just off it. And given that Brady has been embroiled in the "Deflategate" scandal, the Steelers QB might just be taking his spot.

Asked if he tries to break in balls, Roethlisberger replied, "Not me. I never have. . . I just go play."

Of course. Roethlisberger has always played his best when the pressure is high.

CAREER HIGHLIGHTS

- Three-time Pro Bowl selection (2007, 2011, 2014)

- NFL Offensive Rookie of the Year (2004)

- Set a new team record and tied for first in the NFL with 4,952 passing yards in 2014

- Franchise leader in career completions (3,157), yards (39,057) and touchdown passes (251)

- Set the NFL record with 13 straight victories in his first season and most games won by a rookie quarterback in league history, and the most wins over the first two seasons (22)

- At age 23, he is the youngest quarterback to ever win the Super Bowl

TONY ROMO

DALLAS COWBOYS
★ ★ ★
QUARTERBACK
9

The quarterback of the Dallas Cowboys is one of the most romantic positions in all of sports, evoking images of a square-jawed hero leading America's Team to the promised land with a star on his helmet and a starlet on his arm. But being put on that pedestal invites onlookers to try and cut you down.

In some ways Tony Romo has lived up to the image, embracing the celebrity lifestyle, dating famous women and playing in meaningful games, but he wasn't born into it. Romo came from humble roots and worked his way to the top, or at least very close to the top.

At Burlington High School in Wisconsin, Romo was a multisport athlete and was All-State in football.

He wasn't a blue-chip prospect but he was determined. As a 15-year-old he rode his banana-seat bike 15 miles in a snowstorm to play basketball, and led his team to a double overtime win.

Romo ended up one tier below the big boys with a partial football scholarship to Eastern Illinois University in Division I-AA. In four years he was named the Ohio Valley Conference Player of the Year three times, won the Walter Payton Award as the best player in Division I-AA and had his number retired — the first time the school had bestowed that honor on a player.

Apparently, scouts missed the ceremony; Romo wasn't drafted and instead signed with the Cowboys as

a free agent in 2003. He then spent three seasons on the sidelines as a third-string quarterback. But in 2006 he spelled Drew Bledsoe, and for the better part of the past decade, he's been one of the most famous — and maligned — athletes in America.

In 2007, his first full season as a starter, Romo led the Cowboys to 13 wins, tying the franchise record for victories in a season and setting the single-season club marks for touchdown passes (36), completions (335), yardage (4,211) and 300-yard games (7).

Befitting the high-profile nature of the team, he quickly rose to prominence with six of his first 11 starts being nationally televised. He also made headlines by dating singer

CAREER HIGHLIGHTS

- Second Team All-Pro (2014)
- Four-time Pro Bowl selection (2006–07, 2009, 2014)
- Second in NFL history in both passer rating (97.6) and fourth quarter rating (102.2)
- Three-time Ohio Valley Conference Player of the Year and Division I-AA All-American (2000–02)
- Walter Payton Award winner as the top player in Division I-AA (2002)

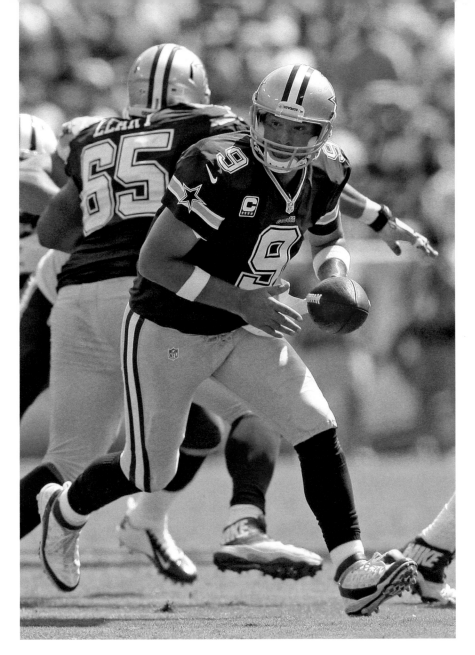

quarterbacks between 1991 and 2013.

If that's not convincing enough for Romo doubters, his career month and year in 2014 should've been. He had his best December, with 12 touchdowns and just one interception, while posting the best passer rating in history (133.7) for a quarterback who averaged at least 25 attempts over four games. For that, he was named the NFC Offensive Player of the Month.

Romo also made his first All-Pro team and his fourth Pro Bowl after throwing for 34 touchdowns and 3,705 yards for the season, while leading the NFL in quarterback rating (113.2), yards per pass average (8.5), completion percentage (69.9), passing touchdown percentage (7.8) and game-winning drives and comebacks (5). The Cowboys won their first NFC East title in five years with a 12-4 record, including four straight wins to end the year and an 8-0 record on the road.

IN THE HUDDLE

At the end of the 2014 season, Romo was first in Cowboys history in career passing yards (33,270), touchdowns (242), yards per game (257.9), quarterback rating (97.6), fourth quarter comebacks (24) and game-winning drives (28).

Jessica Simpson, and by vacationing with her in Mexico a week before a playoff game against the New York Giants. The criticism was withering after the Cowboys lost, and the prevailing opinion was that he didn't have the desire or fortitude to win when it mattered most.

This was reinforced by Romo's late-season play. From 2006 through 2013, in the month of December the Cowboys had a 12-17 record, and Romo threw 27 interceptions. His playoff record was 1-3, with Dallas missing the playoffs five times in that span. The enduring memory of this era is his bobble of a hold for a short field goal that led to a 21–20 loss to the Seattle Seahawks in the 2006 playoffs.

During those years in the wilderness, the old quarterback guard were breaking all-time records, and a new generation of young guns were establishing themselves, giving fans fodder to demand change in Dallas. Romo just kept pedaling against the storm.

Maybe it's cognitive dissonance — when facts conflict with widely held beliefs — but his critics refuse to budge on the false notion that Romo doesn't come through in the clutch. Consider this: in games that are within a touchdown in the fourth quarter, Romo has the league's second-best passer rating and yards per attempt. He is also fourth in touchdown-to-interception ratio and completion percentage among all

In the playoffs Romo led a fourth quarter comeback to beat the Detroit Lions in the wild-card game, and against the Green Bay Packers in the divisional round, he had a 143.6 passer rating on 15 for 19 passing. One of those incompletions was what appeared to be the go-ahead touchdown, but it was called back on a borderline call that cost the Cowboys the game.

There's nothing more Romo could have done, and that kind of finish should truly put perceptions to rest and change the narrative arc of his career. But where's the fun and schadenfreude in that?

"I think people just like rooting," says Romo. "If they like you, they're going to want to root for you, and you're one of theirs. And if they don't like you? It doesn't matter."

MATTHEW STAFFORD

When sports fans endure decades of futility, they tend to blame their luck on supernatural forces. In baseball the Boston Red Sox broke the Curse of the Bambino after 86 years, while the Chicago Cubs are still hexed by a billy goat. The NFL has experienced this otherworldly phenomenon in Detroit, where Lions fans attribute their team's long stretch of misfortune to former quarterback Bobby Layne.

Layne was the last quarterback to win a title for the Lions, a pre–Super Bowl NFL championship in 1957. But in 1958, Lions management decided Layne's playboy lifestyle didn't fit the team image, and he was traded. On his way out of town, he declared that the Lions wouldn't win for the next 50 years. In 2008, on the 50th anniversary of the curse, the Lions secured the dubious distinction of becoming the first team to finish a season 0-16. After the winless year, the Lions, ironically, turned to a graduate of Layne's former high school to help end the jinx.

That man was quarterback Matthew Stafford. As a senior at Highland Park High School in Dallas, Stafford threw for 4,018 yards and 38 touchdowns and led his undefeated team to the state championship.

He played two seasons at the University of Georgia, leading the Bulldogs to two Bowl victories, but some pundits were underwhelmed by his college career. The Lions, however, liked his arm and intelligence and took him with the first pick of the 2009 draft. He won the starting job out of training camp, and in the third game of the season helped the Lions win their first game since 2007 — a 19–14 decision over the Washington Redskins.

Stafford created his own legend later that year in a game against the Cleveland Browns. He was wired for sound by NFL Films while throwing for a then rookie-record 422 yards and tying the rookie single-game record with 5 touchdowns.

IN THE HUDDLE

Stafford set an NFL record for most completions by a quarterback in his first 50 games, with 1,239. He reached 20,000 passing yards in his 71st game, becoming the fastest player in NFL history to reach that mark, and breaking the previous record held by Hall of Famer Dan Marino, who did it in 74 games.

The final touchdown was the most dramatic. Stafford had suffered a shoulder injury on the last play of the game, but the Browns were called for pass interference, and he convinced his coaches to let him throw one more — resulting in a last-second 38–37 victory. Afterward, NFL Films president Steve Sabol said Stafford had "the most dramatic player wiring ever."

His shoulder was re-injured in 2010 and cost him all but three games of the season.

But Stafford came back strong in 2011 with a reconstructed joint, ready to carry the team. A league-high 66.4 percent of their offensive plays were passes, and he set all-time single-season team records in attempts (663), completions (421), yards (5,038), touchdowns (41), completion percentage (63.5 percent) and passer rating (97.2), and was the winner of the NFL's Comeback Player of the Year award.

The Lions made the playoffs for the first time since 1999, but they didn't last long when they ran into Drew Brees and the New Orleans Saints' buzz saw. Stafford threw for 380 yards and 3 touchdowns, but he was intercepted twice, and the Lions lost 45–28.

Including 2011, Stafford has now put up four of the top five single-season passing yard totals in franchise history — with 4,967 in 2012, 4,650 in 2013 and 4,257 in 2014 — and joined Peyton Manning and Hall of Famer Dan Marino as the only quarterbacks in NFL history with four 4,000-yard seasons in their first six years.

Against the Pittsburgh Steelers on November 17, 2013, Stafford threw for 327 yards in the first half, a team record, including a 79-yard touchdown pass to Calvin Johnson. With that, he set a new franchise mark for career passing yards, breaking Layne's record, which stood for 55 years. It was also his 100th touchdown pass in his 55th game, joining Marino, Kurt Warner and Johnny Unitas as the only players in history to throw 100 touchdown passes in their first 55 games.

In 2014 with a lead in the fourth quarter of their wild-card game against the Dallas Cowboys, the Lions looked as though they would get a first down deep in enemy territory after a defensive pass interference call. But the flag was picked up, and the call inexplicably overturned. The Cowboys got the ball back, scored a touchdown and beat the Lions 24–20. The 50 years are up, but Layne's hoodoo seems to linger.

The Lions still have just one playoff victory since 1957 — a 1991 win over the Cowboys — and have lost 11 postseason games in that span. Stafford has now broken just about all of Layne's team records, but Lions fans would prefer he broke Layne's curse.

CAREER HIGHLIGHTS

- Pro Bowl selection (2014)

- NFL Comeback Player of the Year (2011)

- Franchise leader in completions (1,848), yards (21,714) and touchdown passes (131)

- Third quarterback in NFL history with 5,000-plus passing yards and 40-plus touchdowns in a season

- Set the record for most passing yards (422) and touchdowns (5) by a rookie quarterback in a single game (versus Cleveland on November 22, 2009)

RUSSELL WILSON

CAREER HIGHLIGHTS

- Two-time Pro Bowl selection (2012–13)
- Led the NFL in game-winning drives in 2013 and 2014, with five each season
- Holds franchise single-season records for quarterback rating (101.2) and rushing yards (849)
- Winner of the Pro Football Writers of America Good Guy Award (2014)

Russell Carrington Wilson is very much his father's son. Harrison Wilson III, a baseball and football star in high school, woke his son up at 5:30 every morning to run drills. His career as a lawyer taught Russell the power of poise and preparation.

As a senior at private Collegiate High School in Richmond, Virginia, Wilson had over 3,000 yards passing and ran for more than 1,100, while leading his undefeated team to a state title. He also batted .467 on the baseball team, and it was a love of baseball that led to his departure from North Carolina State University.

Wilson was the first freshman quarterback to earn All-ACC honors, but NC State coach Tom O'Brien disagreed with his attending spring training after he was drafted by baseball's Colorado Rockies in 2010. So Wilson transferred to Wisconsin for his final year of eligibility.

Over the course of his collegiate career, Wilson started 50 straight games and set an NCAA record by throwing 379 consecutive passes without an interception. He had a total of 11,720 yards passing and 109 touchdowns, and he rushed for 1,421 yards and 23 touchdowns. At 5-foot-11, however, the knock on Wilson was that he was too short to play quarterback in the NFL. New Seattle Seahawks coach

Pete Carroll and general manager John Schneider saw past that and made him the first quarterback they drafted, taking him in the third round, 75th overall, in 2012.

IN THE HUDDLE

In a 2012 game against Buffalo, Wilson set an NFL record with three rushing touchdowns and a touchdown pass in the first half of a game, while setting franchise quarterback records for most rushing yards (92) and most rushing touchdowns (3) in a game.

Wilson stepped right in, starting all 16 games of his rookie year. He tied Peyton Manning's rookie record with 26 touchdown passes, and set his own by becoming the first rookie quarterback to go undefeated at home and the first to have three straight games with a quarterback rating of 125.0 or higher. He also set franchise quarterback records with a 100.0 rating and 489 rushing yards.

In 2013 the Seahawks won 11 of their first 12 games and the NFC West title. In the playoffs they beat Wilson's childhood hero Drew Brees and the New Orleans Saints, as well as the San Francisco 49ers, to reach Super Bowl XLVIII. Facing the Denver Broncos and Peyton Manning, who was hoping a second championship would cement his

legacy as the NFL's best ever QB, Wilson led the Seahawks to a 43–8 victory. He completed 72 percent of his passes, with two touchdowns and a 123.1 passer rating. It was the franchise's first title and the ultimate validation for Wilson.

In the off-season Wilson hung out with Barack, Bieber, Beyoncé and Ben Haggerty, a.k.a. Seattle rapper Macklemore. There was a bit of a Super Bowl hangover in 2014, and coupled with some internal strife, the Seahawks started 3-3, but the ship was righted and the team finished 12-4. Wilson shattered his own team quarterback record with 849 rushing yards — including three games over 100 yards — while posting the franchise's single-game high of 122 in a game against the Washington Redskins.

Back in the NFC Championship, this time against the Green Bay Packers, the Seahawks were down by 12 with just over two minutes

remaining. Wilson then led one of the most unlikely comebacks in history, including a miraculous two-point conversion, to erase the deficit and win 28–22 on a touchdown pass in overtime.

In Super Bowl XLIX against the New England Patriots, the Seahawks were down by four with 20 seconds left and the ball on the 1-yard line after Wilson calmly marched his team down the field. Poised to score the winning points for back-to-back titles, he was intercepted and the Patriots won 28–24. The play call by coach Carroll to pass instead of giving the ball to running back Marshawn Lynch was called the worst decision by a coach in NFL history. Speaking like a true professional, Wilson took "full responsibility" for the play, while expressing confidence he would lead the team back.

Wilson is often called The

Robot because he's rarely off script, doesn't show any weakness or let the world see past his polish. His recent divorce, for example, is off limits.

Seahawks All-Pro cornerback Richard Sherman, who is the opposite of Wilson in that he speaks his mind off the cuff, says the two really aren't that different. "We're fueled by the same thing. Our whole team is. We're a bunch of underdogs, guys nobody wanted, who didn't fit schemes. That's why he's our leader."

Brees, another undersized quarterback with outsized talent, after whom Wilson has modeled his career, is also a believer. "He's more talented than I am. He's more athletic. He grasped the NFL game at a faster pace than I did. He has not only great leadership qualities, great charisma, but also the it factor that you look for in a young quarterback. I couldn't be more impressed."

RECEIVERS

ODELL BECKHAM JR.

The New York media has been known to create heroes and hype, usually blowing things well beyond proportion to reality. But there was no need to exaggerate on November 23, 2014, and social media took care of the publicity.

It was the day that Odell Beckham Jr. reached behind his head with his back parallel to the ground and snagged an Eli Manning pass with little more than his index finger. He instantly became a sensation.

Beckham was born to perform such feats. The gridiron genetics came from his father, Odell Sr., who was a running back at Louisiana State University, but his speed came from his mom,

Heather Van Norman. She was a six-time track team All-American, and was part of five LSU Lady Tigers track team national championships.

The was little doubt Odell Jr. would go to LSU after graduating from Isidore Newman High School in New Orleans after posting a senior year of 50 receptions for

1,010 yards and 19 touchdowns.

In three seasons in Baton Rouge, Beckham had 143 receptions for 2,340 yards and 12 touchdowns, he returned 42 kickoffs for 1,044 yards (a 24.9-yard average) and had 62 punts for 557 yards and two touchdowns. As a senior he was First Team All-Southeastern Conference and won the Paul Hornung Award as the nation's most versatile player.

After a 7-9 season, the Giants had the 12th overall pick of the 2014 draft and chose Beckham. Slowed by a hamstring tear, he was on the inactive list for the first four games and heard plenty from anxious Giants fans and impatient members of the media.

On October 5 he made his much-anticipated debut at home against the Atlanta Falcons and caught a touchdown pass to put the Giants ahead to stay. Giants leading receiver Victor Cruz tore his patellar tendon the next game, and a week later Beckham had the first of four multi-touchdown games — two against the Dallas Cowboys.

IN THE HUDDLE
In 2014, Beckham joined Hall of Famer Michael Irvin as one of only two players in NFL history with nine straight games of at least 90 receiving yards.

In the ultimate sign of respect, Richard Sherman of the defending champion Seattle Seahawks, one of the very best defensive backs in the game, switched sides to line up against Beckham in Week 10, but Beckham still caught seven passes for 108 yards.

That was just a prelude to what social media deemed the "best catch ever." That kind of hyperbole gets thrown around a lot in the age of instant analysis, but former NFL receiver and NBC analyst Cris Collinsworth called it impossible. "That may be the greatest catch I've ever seen . . . That is absolutely impossible, what he just did."

NFL players and alumni weighed in on Twitter, as did athletes from other sports, celebrities and the non-football media. In the three days following, there were 686,000 mentions, 23,000 tweets per minute and he had 62,726 new followers. The Pro Football Hall of Fame also displayed his jersey.

But Tennessee Titans quarterback Zach Mettenberger, who was Beckham's teammate in college, wasn't as impressed, saying, "He's had better. If you could get your hands on some of the practice film from LSU, you would see what I'm talking about."

Beckham was certainly no one-trick pony that day or any other. He had 10 receptions for 146 yards, which earned him Rookie of the Week honors, and his 38 receptions in the month of November were the second most in the league. In the last game of the season, he had 12 catches for a season-high 185 yards, finishing the year with 1,305 yards.

Beckham led the NFL in yards per game, with 108.8; he was the first receiver in history to reach 1,000 yards after missing the season's first three games (he missed four); and he set NFL records for most catches and yards in the first 12 games of a career.

Beckham also broke Jeremy Shockey's franchise rookie records for receptions and yards receiving, and Bill Swiacki's 1948 rookie record for touchdown receptions. Ultimately, he was named the Offensive Rookie of the Year.

Borrowing a tradition from world football, Beckham traded jerseys with opponents after games, and with one three-fingered catch he joined another Beckham in achieving a level of fame beyond sports. David was alternately built up and cut down by the fickle British media. It remains to be seen how the New York hounds will treat Odell Jr. if he can't live up to one of the greatest debuts in NFL history.

CAREER HIGHLIGHTS

- Pro Bowl selection (2014)
- Offensive Rookie of the Year (2014)
- Led the NFL in receiving yards per game, with 108.8 (2014)
- Set NFL records for most receptions (91) and receiving yards (1,305) in the first 12 games of a career
- Set franchise rookie records for receptions, receiving yards and touchdowns (12)
- Winner of the Paul Hornung Award as the most versatile player in NCAA football (2013)

ANTONIO BROWN

While "Touchdown" Eddie Brown was chasing his professional football dreams and being named best player in Arena Football League history, his son Antonio couch-surfed and occasionally slept in cars in Miami's gritty Liberty City neighborhood, something the younger Brown doesn't like to elaborate on.

"I wasn't a kid who got in trouble or did anything wrong. I just was a guy who didn't really have the right guidance in place and the right support that supported the things that I wanted to do," says Antonio. "It's hard for a kid to be successful when he ain't got the right support to help him be successful."

At Miami's Norland Senior High School, rail-thin Boney Tony was a two-time All-State quarterback and made two 100-meter state finals. Without the test scores to get into college, however, he spent a year at prep school North Carolina Tech, and in five games he threw for 1,247 yards and 11 touchdowns, and had 451 yards and 13 touchdowns rushing.

Florida State University denied Brown admission because of academic concerns, and after a brief stint with Alcorn State University in Mississippi, he walked on at Central Michigan University. Weeks later he was offered a scholarship, and he earned it with 305 career receptions — second in Mid-American Conference history — and was second in CMU history in touchdown receptions (22) and third in receiving yards (3,199). He's the only player in school history to record two 1,000-yard receiving seasons, as well as the only player with two 100-reception seasons. He scored touchdowns receiving, rushing, passing and on punt and kickoff returns.

Brown's talent was raw, however, and he was only 5-foot-10 and 186 pounds, so he lasted until the sixth round of the 2010 draft. The Pittsburgh Steelers selected him 195th overall, and he had to work his way up the depth chart, even after taking the opening kickoff of his first game 89 yards for a touchdown after a handoff. He was inactive for seven games in his rookie year and caught only 16 passes.

"You've got to be patient," said Brown. "Patience builds perseverance and it builds humility and it teaches you a lot. I just had to go through that."

It paid off in the 2010 playoffs, when Brown made two YouTube-worthy catches that cemented his place in the hearts of Pittsburgh fans and management. The first catch, which he pinned to his helmet to secure, set the stage for the winning points against the Baltimore Ravens in the divisional round. The second one he caught on his knees to seal a victory over the New York Jets and send the Steelers to Super Bowl XLV.

IN THE HUDDLE

In 2013, Brown became the first player in NFL history to have at least five receptions and 50 receiving yards in all 16 games of a regular season, which he did again in 2014.

The Steelers lost to the Green Bay Packers, but Brown had established himself and would go from part-time player to record breaker in one season. In 2011 he set a new team mark with 2,211 all-purpose yards — 1,062 on returns and 1,108 receiving; he was the first player in NFL history with at least 1,000 receiving yards and 1,000 return yards in the same season; and he was picked for the Pro Bowl as a kick returner and named Steelers MVP.

"I love him," said former teammate Hines Ward. "I'm not surprised. He was always full of talent. It was just a matter of learning the system."

With the system learned and mastered, in 2013 Brown broke the 16-year-old single-season franchise record with 1,499 receiving yards and had the second-most receptions (110) in team history. The following season he blew those away, leading the NFL with 1,698 yards and 129 receptions, which broke Ward's 2002 team record by 17 catches and was the second-highest single-season total in league history. He also became only the fourth player in NFL history with at least 110 receptions in two straight seasons.

Brown's 13 receiving touchdowns in 2014 also set a franchise mark, and he still returned kicks, taking one back 71 yards for another touchdown. He now has three of the top-4 single-season all-purpose yard totals in the team's long and storied history.

"He's got the best hands and feet working together on the sideline or in the back of the end zone of anyone I've ever seen," said quarterback Ben Roethlisberger.

Offensive lineman Ramon Foster concurs. "His work ethic is the best, bar none. If you see him practice, you can understand his production. He's the standard for the wide receiver position."

DEZ BRYANT

You can't judge Dez Bryant until you've run a mile in his shoes — as hard as that would be. The rush to judgment of his character has been quicker than his ascent up the Cowboys' receiving record books, but it helps to know where he comes from before casting stones.

Born in Galveston County, Texas, Bryant had 101 receptions for 2,232 yards and 37 touchdowns in his final two seasons at Lufkin High School. He also upped his grades in the latter part of high school, pulling himself out of special education so he could qualify for college admission.

"I've taught school for 35 years, and I've never been prouder of a student than I am of him," says Jody Anderson, Bryant's math teacher. "I admired what he was trying to do and how hard he worked to do it."

Courted by all the NCAA heavyweight teams of the region, Bryant chose Oklahoma State University because he believed they showed him the most support. After being a consensus All-American in his sophomore season he was a favorite to win the Heisman Trophy as a junior. It was a truncated year, however.

Introduced to former Dallas Cowboy Deion Sanders by mutual friend Michael Crabtree, Bryant lied about a lunch he had with the Hall of Famer, thinking it violated NCAA rules. It didn't, but the lie was enough to get him suspended for the majority of his junior year.

Instead of being one of the first off the board when he declared for the draft, Bryant fell to the bottom of the first round. The Cowboys traded up three spots to take him 24th overall in 2010.

Leading up to the draft, he also couldn't escape the shadow of his mother, Angela, who had been in prison for selling drugs in 1997 and was arrested again for possession in 2009, for which she received ten years of probation.

IN THE HUDDLE
From 2012 through 2014, Bryant had three of the top-10 seasons in franchise history in receptions, receiving yards and receiving touchdowns.

"The reason my mom sold drugs and went to jail is so we could live," Bryant said. "She paid a hard price for it. Now she doesn't ever have to do anything like that again. God put me in this position to help my family and others who have helped me."

Angela was only 15 when she had Desmond, and his youth was transient, living with various relatives and friends. It was further complicated when she came out as a lesbian while he was in high school, not an easy

thing to do in a small Bible Belt town.

In 2012, Bryant was arrested for allegedly assaulting his mother, charges which were conditionally dismissed. It led to the Cowboys creating the "Dez Rules," including a midnight curfew, no alcohol, weekly counseling sessions, and a team security official accompanying him to nightclubs and driving him to all team activities.

Whether it was the conditions placed on him by the team or his own maturity as a player or person, from 2012 to 2014 Bryant became a superstar. Over those three seasons he had 273 receptions for 3,935 yards and 41 touchdowns. In 2014 he had 16 receiving touchdowns to lead the league and break the Cowboys' single-season mark, he was a First Team All-Pro, and he made his second consecutive Pro Bowl.

Bryant was a key cog in the Cowboys' potent attack, and it was his mastery of skill that nearly had the Cowboys in the conference championships. With less than five minutes to play against the Green

Bay Packers in the divisional playoffs, Bryant made a miraculous, one-handed catch on fourth down that appeared to everyone but the replay officials to be a touchdown. The score would have put the Cowboys ahead, but it was ruled that Bryant didn't have control throughout his roll into the end zone. The Packers got the ball back on downs and never gave it up. It was a controversial call that ended the Cowboys' 2014 season, but it wasn't the last controversy involving Bryant.

Rumors of an incriminating video of Bryant swirled in the off-season. The video is believed to show a domestic incident in a Walmart parking lot, and people from Byrant's past were using it to blackmail him. The

stories stalled negotiations with the Cowboys, who gave him the franchise tag to keep him with the team.

Bryant's upbringing is an explanation, not an excuse, but the Cowboys were confident enough in his actions and in his ability to separate himself from old friends and advisors to lift the Dez Rules in 2015.

"He'll be the first to tell you that a big part of why he has evolved is because he's had great support, he's had great encouragement, he's had great understanding," said team owner Jerry Jones.

It will be Bryant's turn now to prove to everyone that, left unchecked, he can be as responsible off the field as he is explosive on it.

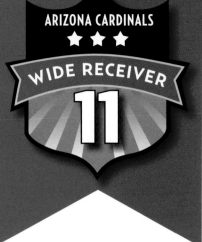

ARIZONA CARDINALS

★ ★ ★

WIDE RECEIVER

11

LARRY
FITZGERALD

Known as Spidey for his sticky palms that reel in footballs at a record-setting rate, Larry Fitzgerald is regarded as one of the league's best-conditioned and most elegant players. However, he could just as easily be called Wolverine for being impervious to pain. His two historic catching streaks, despite serious injuries to his superhero hands, attest to that characteristic.

The 6-foot-3, 218-pound Minnesota native had his first magical run while playing for the University of Pittsburgh Panthers. Fitzgerald was a sophomore in 2002, and he hauled in 92 receptions for 1,672 yards and 22 touchdowns. His performance earned him the Walter Camp Award as the best player in NCAA football as well as the Biletnikoff Award as top wide receiver — all while playing with a torn ligament in his right hand.

That season, Fitzgerald became the first player in Panthers history with back-to-back years totaling over 1,000 yards receiving, and when he left Pittsburgh after just two years, he held the school record of 34 touchdowns.

Fitzgerald's second streak came in 2008 while playing for the Arizona Cardinals, who drafted him 3rd overall in 2004. Fitzgerald had proven himself a bona fide NFL star in Phoenix, when in 2005 he became the youngest receiver in league history — at 22 years and 123 days — with 100 receptions. He ended up with 103, setting the Arizona franchise record. But in 2008 he embarked on something extra special. In the regular season he became the fourth receiver in NFL history (after Jerry Rice, Marvin Harrison and Randy Moss) to have at least 1,400 receiving yards in three or more seasons, which was a fitting entrance for what was going to be a postseason for the ages.

In Arizona's quest for a championship, Fitzgerald set all-time NFL playoff marks for catches (30), yards (546), touchdowns (7) and TD catches in consecutive games (4). And it wasn't easy. After being held in check by the Pittsburgh Steelers for much of Super Bowl XLIII, Fitzgerald took over in the last 11 minutes, catching six passes for 115 yards and two touchdowns. Fitzgerald's second TD, a 64-yard catch-and-run from quarterback Kurt Warner, gave the Cardinals a 23–20 lead with 2:37 left.

But Arizona's luck had run out, and Steelers QB Ben Roethlisberger marched his team down the field and scored with 35 seconds left. Although Fitzgerald had one more catch, the Cardinals' final drive ended when Warner was sacked and fumbled the ball with five seconds left.

It was later revealed that Fitzgerald had played through a broken left thumb and torn cartilage in his left hand between his middle and ring fingers. Still, he went to the Pro Bowl following the Super Bowl and was named the game's MVP.

Like Spiderman and other superheroes whose backstories are often marked by tragic circumstances that serve as impetus and inspiration, Fitzgerald too has had to deal with adversity at home.

In 2003 his mother died of a brain aneurysm while fighting breast cancer. Fitzgerald hasn't cut his hair since, and braids it in tribute to her.

The Cardinals have been without a star quarterback since Kurt Warner retired after the 2009 season, but Fitzgerald has still set records for being the youngest player to reach 11,000 yards, 80 touchdowns and 900 receptions. The mind boggles imagining what the numbers would be if he'd been paired with a Tom Brady or Drew Brees.

In 2014, Fitzgerald finally had a worthy passer when Carson Palmer resurrected his career. But then Palmer went down with an injury, and his backup and then the backup to the backup all got hurt. With the quarterback carousel and ligament and MCL injuries hampering Fitzgerald, his numbers were slightly below his stellar career averages, but the Cardinals went 11-6 and made the playoffs, losing in the wild card to the Carolina Panthers.

With a $120 million contract that ran through the 2018 season, Arizona was confident putting the future of the franchise in Fitzgerald's Hall of Fame–bound hands. He showed his commitment by giving millions back before the 2015 season

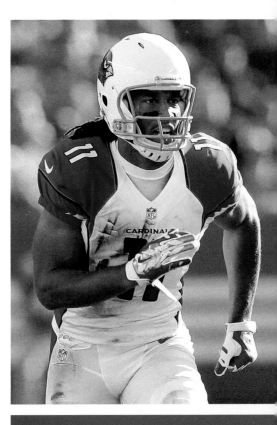

CAREER HIGHLIGHTS

- Eight-time Pro Bowl selection (2005, 2007–13)

- Holds the all-time record for Pro Bowl touchdowns (8)

- First Team All-Pro (2008)

- Two-time Second Team All-Pro selection (2009, 2011)

- Set the NFL single postseason record for receptions (30), receiving yards (546) and receiving touchdowns (7) in 2008

- Had nine TD receptions in six career postseason games, an NFL record for a player in his first six postseason games

- Cardinals career leader in receptions (909), receiving yards (12,151), touchdowns (89) and 100-yard receiving games (38)

to help the Cardinals stay under the salary cap and sign new players.

Superhuman catching ability, humility and generosity — that kind of character usually exists only in fiction.

SAN DIEGO CHARGERS
★ ★ ★
TIGHT END
85

ANTONIO GATES

At Central High School in Detroit, Antonio Gates was First Team All-State in both football and basketball, leading his team to the state championship in the latter in his senior year. Basketball meant so much to him that he left Michigan State University when they insisted he focus on football. He ended up at Kent State, where he became a hardcourt legend.

In Gates' two seasons with the Golden Flashes, the team won back-to-back conference championships and made it to the Elite Eight of the NCAA tournament in 2002. He graduated as Kent State's sixth all-time leading scorer, and his number, 44, was retired. That wasn't enough to convince NBA scouts, however, who believed the 6-foot-4 power forward didn't have the height to succeed professionally. So in the summer of 2003, he scheduled his own workout for NFL teams. Unbeknownst to most of the personnel there, he'd sprained his ankle in a basketball game a week prior, which explained his less-than-impressive showing.

Tim Brewster, the Chargers tight ends coach at the time, knew about the ankle and had seen enough of Gates — on the basketball court. "If I had been truthful to the organization about what I saw that day," says Brewster, "we probably wouldn't have signed Antonio." But they did, and the $7,000 signing bonus was probably the best money the team ever spent.

Gates hadn't played a down of football since high school, but it took all of one season to shake off the rust and master the position. In 2004, his second season,

CAREER HIGHLIGHTS

- Three-time First Team All-Pro selection (2004–06)

- Two-time Second Team All-Pro selection (2009–10)

- Eight-time Pro Bowl selection (2004–11)

- NFL's 2000s All-Decade Team (Second Team)

- Active NFL leader in career touchdowns (99)

- Holds franchise records for receptions (788), receiving yards (10,014) and touchdowns (99)

he had 81 receptions for 964 yards and set the single-season touchdown record for tight ends, with 13. He was named starter for the Pro Bowl and a First Team All-Pro.

Having Drew Brees at quarterback in San Diego helped Gates' early development, but he hardly missed a step when Brees left town. Philip Rivers took over at quarterback in 2006, and Gates made the Pro Bowl and All-Pro teams again that season. Their partnership has flourished ever since. In 2011 they became the quarterback–tight end duo with the most touchdowns in NFL history.

IN THE HUDDLE

Among tight ends, Gates is fourth in NFL history in receptions and receiving yards, second in first downs and touchdowns, and first in catches of 25-plus yards.

Gates is a nightmare to defensively match up against. He's too strong for cornerbacks and too quick for linebackers and safeties. Now that he's a veteran, he's also stopped relying solely on his freakish talent and become a more cerebral player, something he was forced to do in 2010 when a torn plantar fascia in his right foot spoiled the record-setting pace he was on. He still managed to have ten touchdowns in ten games to lead the team and be a Pro Bowler and All-Pro yet again.

"You can only do so much physically," says Gates. "You can only run so fast and jump so high. Mentally there is an unlimited capacity on how you can grow. Mentally the game seems slower."

Any questions about Gates' performance as he gets older were quickly put to rest with the nine touchdowns he scored in the

Chargers' first eight games of 2014, which tied a team record. He ended the season with 12, one short of his career-high 2004 total, and tied with young guns Rob Gronkowski and Julius Thomas for the league lead among tight ends.

At the end of the year, Gates had career totals of 788 receptions for 10,014 yards and 99 touchdowns, all franchise records, and he and Rivers have extended their NFL record for a quarterback–tight end tandem to 72 touchdowns. Gates is also the active NFL leader in career touchdowns, with ten more than second place Larry Fitzgerald.

Signed through 2015, if his 13th season is his last, there's nothing left for Gates to accomplish, except to bring San Diego its first Super Bowl. But he's thinking of a life and legacy beyond football.

"You've been competing and traveling for so many years.

Then all of the sudden you're going to be sitting at home and feel like you're not yourself. You'll feel like you're not contributing . . . I'm terrified of having that feeling."

So Gates will return to the Motor City and try to bring boxing back to its former glory, while providing opportunities in a city with few to offer. His paternal grandfather, Henry Hank, was a boxer in the 1950s and 60s who had 97 professional bouts, and Gates attended fights as a boy, admiring local legends like Tommy Hearns.

"Growing up in Detroit isn't always easy," says Gates, who became a licensed promoter and manager in 2013. "I know what it's like to want to be somebody, and I know what it's like to become somebody. That's why I'm doing this. If I can get one kid off the streets or help one kid start his career or have a role in one kid becoming a man, then it's worth it."

JIMMY GRAHAM

When Jimmy Graham was 11 years old, his mother decided she couldn't raise all her children alone. So, with two garbage bags of clothes to his name, Graham was left by his mother on the doorstep of a group home. Graham wasn't a troublemaker, but this home was for teens who had broken the law.

"Waking up in a place you don't know, with people you don't know, getting beat up every day — it sculpted me," says Graham. "I battled, but it's made my character." Graham had to fight for his food and often went without, so when he discovered a local church meeting that gave out free food, he jumped at the chance to become involved.

Teaching the Bible classes was Becky Vinson, a young single mother trying to pay her

way through school. She took Graham under her wing and eventually welcomed him into her home. "It wasn't like I was trying to harbor someone's kid," Vinson says. "He'd come eat and absolutely didn't want to go home . . . In the winter, Jimmy would come to the house in shorts and kneesocks. He had only three sets of clothes and one pair of pants. He had holes in his shoes."

Vinson pushed Graham to work on his grades, which kept him on North Carolina's Charis Prep School basketball team and earned him a scholarship to the University of Miami, where he earned a business degree with a double major in marketing and management and was a two-time Academic All-ACC selection.

IN THE HUDDLE
Since 2013, no tight end has had more touchdowns (26), receptions (171) or receiving yards (2,104) than Graham.

Hurricanes basketball coach Frank Haith called Graham the best post defender he ever had — his 104 blocked shots are a testament to that — and he was offered tryouts with nine NBA teams and a basketball contract in Spain. He also got a call from the New England Patriots, even though he hadn't played a down of football since ninth grade.

Miami's football coaches had also taken note of his rare blend of size, speed, toughness and soft hands. With the help of university president Donna Shalala, Graham was convinced to take graduate courses and play a season of college football. Shalala called in former Hurricanes quarterback and NFL All-Pro Bernie Kosar to tutor Graham on the field.

"I could throw it 11 feet in the air, and he'd still jump up 12

feet to get it," says Kosar. "I kept telling him, 'Jimmy, not only are you going to be a great player, you're going to be a superstar.' "

In his one season at Miami, Graham had a relatively modest 17 receptions with a 12.5-yard average, but he was saved for the red zone, and his first three catches were all touchdowns. The New Orleans Saints saw the raw potential and drafted him in 95th overall in 2010.

After scoring five touchdowns in his rookie year, Graham spent the off-season honing his craft with quarterback Drew Brees and other Saints teammates. The hard work paid off. In 2011, Graham was second in receptions in the NFC, and he surpassed Kellen Winslow's single-season NFL tight end yardage record (1,290), finishing with 1,310 yards — but so did the Patriots' Rob Gronkowski, who set the new record with 17 more yards than Graham.

The two tight ends have helped redefine the position. In 2013, Graham lined up in the traditional tight end position only 33.3 percent of the time, and he led the Saints in receptions (86), yards (1,215) and touchdowns (16). Trying to keep him from free agency in 2014, the Saints put the franchise tag on Graham, triggering a salary based on an average of the top players at his position. It meant he would

make about $5 million a year less than he would have as a receiver, so he filed a grievance. The league arbitrator ruled against Graham's petition based on his "physical attributes and skill sets." The Saints later signed him to a four-year, $40 million contract, but one year later he was gone.

The Seattle Seahawks, who missed out on winning their second consecutive Super Bowl because of an ill-conceived pass from the 1-yard line, needed a reliable red zone threat. No Seahawk had more than six red zone touchdown receptions over the past two seasons, while 20 of Graham's 26 touchdowns over that time were from 20 yards or fewer. Seattle decided to trade for the player they needed: they parted with starting center Max Unger as well as a first-round pick in 2015.

The trade shocked the NFL, upset Brees and the Saints players, and gave an already potent lineup an almost unstoppable touchdown machine.

His new team and city couldn't be more excited.

CINCINNATI BENGALS
★ ★ ★
WIDE RECEIVER
18

A.J. GREEN

Woodrow and Dora Green taught humility and the value of hard work to their son Adriel Jeremiah. For over a quarter century in Summerville, South Carolina, Woodrow pulled triple shifts at a steel mill while Dora worked at Walmart. They also taught A.J. to honor his commitments, such as the one he made to the University of Georgia before his junior year at Summerville High School.

After Green was named All-State for the third and fourth times, all the major programs came calling, and Green was pressured to attend the University of South Carolina. Basketball coach and mentor Louis Mulkey took him to Athens to visit the Georgia campus, where he'd already pledged to go, and encouraged him to choose his own path.

Mulkey had taken five-year-old A.J. under his wing after his older brother, Avionce, died in a car accident that also paralyzed his aunt but left A.J. unscathed.

Mulkey didn't get to see the collegiate star Green became, however. He was one of the Charleston Nine who perished in a warehouse fire — the worst loss of lives for American firefighters since 9/11. Green and the Summerville basketball team dedicated their season to Mulkey, and won the school's first state title with a one-point victory in the title game.

In three seasons and just 32 games on the gridiron at Summerville, Green ranked third in school history in receptions (166) and receiving yards (2,619), was second in receiving touchdowns (23), and made the academic honor roll.

University of Georgia coach Mark Richt, who attended Mulkey's funeral, was there for both Green's successes and trials. "He's a very humble kid. He loves his teammates. He wants to win. You know, when you have some of your greatest players be guys that care about the team and are willing to work and pay the price and be there when he doesn't have to be there, that's pretty important."

With an excellent reputation and sterling numbers as a Bulldog, the Cincinnati Bengals drafted him with the fourth overall pick in 2011, one round before they chose quarterback Andy Dalton. The two had instant chemistry. In a game against Denver, they became the first rookie quarterback–wide receiver tandem in NFL history to have 10 completions in a game, and they led the Bengals to the playoffs for just the third time since 1990.

In Green's NFL debut he had the longest game-winning touchdown catch in NFL history by a rookie playing in his team's season opener, and by the end of the season he led the Bengals and all NFL rookies in receptions (65) and receiving yards (1,057). In his second year he became the second player in 48 seasons to score in nine

CAREER HIGHLIGHTS

- Two-time Second Team All-Pro selection (2012–13)
- Four-time Pro Bowl selection (2011–14)
- Holds franchise records with touchdowns in nine straight games and five consecutive games of 100-plus yards receiving

straight games, and Hall of Fame receiver Michael Irvin called him "the best all-around receiver in the National Football League."

In 2013, Green's 1,426 receiving yards were only 14 behind Chad Johnson's franchise record, and he had accumulated more receiving yards than any player in NFL history over their first three seasons.

The 2014 season was his most difficult. He missed three games and was limited in others with turf toe, an arm injury and a concussion in the final quarter of the regular season, which caused him to sit out the Bengals wild-card playoff loss to the Indianapolis Colts. He still led the team in receptions (69), receiving yards (1,041) and receiving touchdowns (six), and he had five 100-yard games, including a career-high 224 yards against Pittsburgh, the second-highest total in franchise history.

IN THE HUDDLE

In 2012, Green became the first player in NFL history to have 100 receptions, 1,500 yards receiving and 10 touchdowns in his first 20 NFL games, and he had more receptions over his first three seasons than anyone in NFL history.

Even after an injury-plagued 2014, his 329 receptions trailed only Anquan Boldin (342) and Larry Fitzgerald (330) for the most over a player's first four years. His 4,874 yards are fourth all-time over the same span, behind Randy Moss (5,396), Torry Holt (5,088) and Jerry Rice (4,881). He has also been in the Pro Bowl every year.

The Bengals have also made the playoffs in each of Green's four seasons, but they're still awaiting their first postseason victory since 1990. The team picked up the fifth-year option on his contract for 2015, as the two sides work out a long-term deal.

"I play this game not just because of the money, man," said Green. "I play because one day I want to put on that Hall of Fame jacket. Also, I want a Super Bowl. The money is just going to come anyway. But if you're not happy, the money really doesn't mean anything."

Green knows there are far more important things in life, and as his mother told him, "You control the money. Don't let the money control you. Spend it wisely."

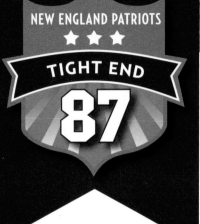

ROB GRONKOWSKI

Head coach Bill Belichick runs the New England Patriots with very little room for dissension or individuality among players — kind of like a military unit. This makes them one of the least colorful teams in the NFL, but when it comes to New England's 6-foot-6, 265-pound tight end, Belichick lets Gronk dance to his own beat, usually without a shirt on.

If Rob Gronkowski wasn't such a devastating force or "pieced together by the football gods," as former wide receiver Nate Burleson described him, then Belichick might make him toe the line.

In a shortened two-year stint at the University of Arizona, Gronkowski had more receptions (75), receiving yards (1,197) and touchdowns (16) than any tight end in Wildcats history. He set the records in only 22 games because back surgery forced him to miss the entire 2009 season, which lowered

his stock and his draft position. The Patriots chose Gronkowski in the second round, 42nd overall, in 2010 after Belichick got an honest and positive assessment from Arizona coach Mike Stoops. "Don't get lost in his awkward silliness," Stoops said. "It's not immaturity. He's a great competitor."

His surgery and draft position didn't affect him in his rookie year in 2010. Gronkowski's 10 touchdowns set team records for tight ends and first-year players at any position, and were the second most by a rookie tight end in NFL history. His sophomore season, however, was one for the ages.

Gronkowski broke the 30-year tight end receiving yards record with 1,327 yards, and shattered the tight end touchdown record of 13, with 17 receiving and 18 total.

IN THE HUDDLE

Gronkowski is the first tight end in NFL history with three straight seasons of 10-plus touchdowns (2010–12) and four overall, and the fastest to record 50 touchdown catches.

Gronkowski didn't stop scoring in the playoffs. He tied an NFL postseason tight end record with three touchdowns in the Patriots' 45–10 rout of the Denver Broncos in the divisional playoffs, and had five catches for 87 yards in the AFC Championship win over Baltimore. On his last catch, his ankle twisted grotesquely, and the high ankle sprain became one of the top storylines leading up to the Super Bowl.

Loaded with pain killers and with his ankle heavily taped, Gronkowski hobbled the entire game, and it may have cost the Patriots the Super Bowl. Down 21–17, Tom Brady's last-second Hail Mary pass was deflected in the end zone and fell just out of Gronkowski's reach after he raced halfway down the field on one

functional foot.

Hours after the game, he was caught on camera dancing shirtless, leading to questions about his commitment and the injury. Said former Patriots safety and NBC analyst Rodney Harrison, "When we lost the Super Bowl . . . I was so devastated the last thing I ever wanted to do was party . . . It's just immaturity. It's not right."

But Gronkowski wasn't faking the surgery he had days later, the first of six that would follow and hamper his next two seasons.

In November 2012, Gronkowski broke his forearm blocking a punt and broke it again the following January. An infection caused him to miss the first six games of the 2013 season, and in the off-season, he had surgery to repair a herniated disk in his back. When he finally returned, he tore his ACL and MCL on a hit that also caused him to lose consciousness. He missed a total of 17 games over the two seasons.

His recovery from the knee operation proved that Gronk isn't your average human, as his leg lost almost no muscle mass postsurgery. He committed to rehab the way he commits to a keg, occasionally doing both. He recovered in Miami, where he enjoyed the nightlife but never missed his 7 a.m. therapy sessions, and he returned to the field ahead of schedule.

The Patriots started 2014 slowly as Gronkowski eased back into the lineup, but as he heated up so did the team, averaging 34.5 points per game compared to 17.8 when he was out. He finished the season with 82 receptions, led all tight ends with 1,124 yards and 12 touchdowns, and was named Comeback Player of the Year. He was also a First Team All-Pro for the first time since 2011 — there was no Second Team player

CAREER HIGHLIGHTS

- Two-time First Team All-Pro selection (2011, 2014)

- Three-time Pro Bowl selection (2011–12, 2014)

- Comeback Player of the Year (2014)

- Led the NFL in receiving touchdowns (17) in 2011 and set the NFL single-season tight end records for receiving yards (1,327), receiving touchdowns and total touchdowns (18)

because he received every vote – and the season had its fairy tale ending.

In Super Bowl XLIX, Gronkowski had a touchdown reception and came through with two catches for 33 yards late in the fourth quarter on the go-ahead touchdown drive, and the Patriots held on for a 28–24 victory. You're allowed to dance when you win it all, and this time Gronk brought Patriots owner Robert Kraft onstage with Flo Rida and Rick Ross, and he kept his shirt on.

That's growth.

T.Y. HILTON

INDIANAPOLIS COLTS
★ ★ ★
WIDE RECEIVER
13

CAREER HIGHLIGHTS

- Pro Bowl selection (2014)

- Holds Colts records for receptions (13) and receiving yards (224) in a postseason game, and yards in a single postseason (327)

- Sun Belt Conference Player of the Year (2010)

- Ranked fifth in NCAA history with 7,498 career all-purpose yards

His name is Eugene. His parents call him by his middle name, Marquise, and the football world knows him as T.Y. because his dad, Tyrone, was his coach in the Gwen Cherry Park youth football league in Miami, where the people called Eugene Little T.Y. Don't confuse that with Ty; that's his brother's name.

Little T.Y. grew up in Liberty City, which also gave the world superstar receivers Santana Moss and Chad "Ochocinco" Johnson. When he got a little bigger, he was named Dade County Athlete of the Year and First Team All-Dade in his senior year at Miami Springs High School, after catching 42 passes for 785 yards and 16 touchdowns, along with four kick return touchdowns.

Hilton chose Florida International University over national powerhouse West Virginia. His deciding factor? When he placed the hats of each school on his bed, his newborn son, Eugene, repeatedly chose the FIU hat.

"That was a win over some of the bigger schools in America," said coach Mario Cristobal. "It's a tribute to him wanting to be a guy that sets his own footprints and doesn't follow anybody else's footsteps. It's a tribute to him for believing in his hometown to start a Division I program and needing

a guy to be the face of the program. That's a lot for a 17- or 18-year-old to put on his shoulders."

Hilton's first touch was a 74-yard punt return for a touchdown, and by the end of his collegiate career, he had rewritten the school and Sun Belt Conference record book, setting the marks for receptions (229), receiving yards (3,351), touchdown receptions (24), kick return yards (2,855) and touchdowns (4), all-purpose yards (7,498), and total touchdowns (37).

But at 5-foot-9, 178 pounds, from a mid-major conference and hampered by a torn quadriceps during his Pro Day workouts, Hilton wasn't drafted until the third round, 92nd overall, by the Indianapolis Colts in 2012. It was a productive draft for Indy that was structured around first overall pick Andrew Luck.

With the new tandem and some help from veteran receiver Reggie Wayne — who is 11 years older than Hilton but with a similar style and build and mutual friends in Florida — the Colts' rebuild was swift.

Wayne, who was mentored by Marvin Harrison after being drafted in 2001, was happy to help his new protégé, and Hilton became his shadow, jotting down lessons in a notepad. Having a dual receiving threat helped the rookie quarterback and spread the defense. After a

down year in 2011, Wayne had 106 catches in 2012, while Hilton had 50 receptions and seven touchdowns to lead all rookies and the Colts. Hilton also set a franchise rookie record with five 100-yard receiving games.

Wayne could no longer draw coverage after he tore his ACL in 2013, but Hilton thrived in the role of primary receiver with Wayne on the sideline offering tips and encouragement. In the 11 games Hilton played without Wayne, he had 998 yards — a third of the team's receiving total — and his 72 receptions were almost twice as many as the team's next leading receiver.

In 2014, Hilton was sixth in the NFL with 1,345 yards, three spots behind childhood friend Antonio Brown of the Pittsburgh Steelers, who also grew up in Liberty City and played in the Gwen Cherry league. Both are under 6 feet tall but thrive in a position that demands height.

"Antonio Brown is a fabulous football player, and T.Y. is much the same," says Colts coach Chuck Pagano. "They're game wreckers. They have great awareness, instincts, athletic ability and the ability to take the top off the defense. They're dynamic. They have feet like a shore bird, quicker than hiccups. . . Even though they're small in stature, they play big."

IN THE HUDDLE
Hilton set the Colts' record for the most receiving yards (1,944) and 100-yard games (10) in a player's first two seasons with the team, and became just the sixth player in NFL history with ten 100-yard receiving games in the first two seasons of their career.

And The Ghost, as Pagano nicknamed Hilton, is a big-game player. The Colts have made the playoffs in each of his three years. In the 2013 wild-card game against the Kansas City Chiefs, he set franchise postseason single-game records with 13 catches and 224 yards. His totals represented the second-most receptions in a single NFL playoff game and the third-most yards. He was the second player in team postseason history to finish a game with 200-plus receiving yards — after Wayne, of course — and set a team record for a single postseason with 327 receiving yards in just two games.

Another big game was played on November 23, 2014, hours after wife Shantrell gave birth to daughter Eugenia. Hilton caught a 73-yard touchdown in a 23–3 win over the Jacksonville Jaguars. He cradled the ball in his arms like a baby in celebration, gave a tearful TV interview after the game, and then brought his new daughter the game ball as he'd promised Shantrell.

He got close, but he couldn't bring her a Super Bowl trophy too. After their third consecutive 11-5 season in 2014, the Colts beat former teammate Manning and the Broncos in Denver before losing to the eventual Super Bowl champion New England Patriots in the AFC Championship. With two of the NFL's most exciting young offensive talents and an ageless wonder guiding them, a second Super Bowl to add to their 2006 title is in their sights.

"It's exciting," says Hilton of the Colts' new generation. "Coming in here with Andrew, I just pictured us becoming like Marvin, Peyton and Reggie."

DETROIT LIONS
★ ★ ★
WIDE RECEIVER
81

CALVIN JOHNSON

After cycling through a few nicknames in his nascent career, then Lions teammate Roy Williams dubbed Calvin Johnson "Megatron," to urge the humble superstar to morph into a machine on the field.

"He always had a kind nature" says Johnson's mother, Arica, who has a PhD and works for the Atlanta school system. "He was the one to pick [opponents] off the ground. Sportsmanship was important to him."

Armed with poise, impressive grades and a complete physical package, Johnson had his pick of schools but chose to stay in his home state and go to Georgia Tech. In his second game he became a Yellow Jackets legend for scoring two touchdowns in the final two minutes to beat Clemson.

"God touched him in so many different ways," said Buddy Geis, the receivers coach at Georgia Tech. "But Calvin works like He didn't give him anything."

After setting most of Georgia Tech's receiving records,

being named an All-American twice, and the ACC Player of the Year, and winning the Biletnikoff Award, Johnson left after his junior season and was taken second overall by the Detroit Lions in 2007.

The Lions were awful, and in his second year they became the first franchise to finish a season 0-16. But they had Johnson, who led the league in receiving touchdowns (12) in 2008. He managed this with five different quarterbacks, none of whom had an accuracy rate above 60 percent.

IN THE HUDDLE
Since entering the NFL in 2007, Johnson is first in the league in receiving yards (10,405), receiving touchdowns (74) and receptions of 25-plus yards (93), and he's the only player in NFL history to have over 5,000 yards receiving in a three-year span (2011–13).

Not one for self-aggrandizement and on a losing team, Johnson quietly went about building a strong résumé and working hard on the practice field, with the trainers, and in the yoga studio. It earned him respect league wide.

Johnson led the NFL in receiving yards (1,681) in 2011, including the highest single-game total of the year (244), and joined Randy Moss as the only receiver with over 1,600 yards and 16-plus touchdowns in one season. And he shone when the season's spotlight was at its brightest: in the first playoff game of his career, he had 12 receptions for 211 yards and 2 touchdowns. The New Orleans Saints outgunned the Lions 45–28, but it was the third time in four games Johnson went over 200 yards receiving. In the process, he set the NFL record for receiving yards in the wild-card round of the playoffs and for the Lions' franchise in the postseason.

That was a prelude to 2012, when Johnson hit a level unseen in league history. He set records by being the first player with eight straight games over 100 yards receiving, the first to play four consecutive games with 10-plus receptions, and he broke the single-season record with 1,964 yards, surpassing Jerry Rice's 1995 record by 116 yards after getting 225 yards in the second-last game of the season.

Johnson almost added the single-game record in 2013 with 329 yards against the Dallas Cowboys. It was the second-highest total in NFL history and the most in regulation time, and in 2014 he went over 10,000 career yards in his 115th game to set a new NFL record for the quickest to 10,000, one game less than Torry Holt.

Signed through 2019, Johnson's next accomplishment will be to transform the Lions into a Super Bowl team. With a second playoff loss in 2014, he risks joining Lions running

CAREER HIGHLIGHTS

- Three-time First Team All-Pro selection (2011–13)

- Second Team All-Pro (2010)

- Five-time Pro Bowl selection (2012–14)

- Holds the NFL single-season record for receiving yards, with 1,964 (2012)

- Holds franchise career records for receiving yards, receiving touchdowns and yards per game, with 10,405, 74 and 87.4, respectively, at the end of the 2014 season

back Barry Sanders as one of the best players in NFL history who built their Hall of Fame credentials in the regular season, a dubious distinction for the franchise.

Meanwhile, Johnson will continue to work as hard as an undrafted rookie and earn admiration from teammates and trash-talking opponents alike. "Scottie Pippen and those guys talk about how there would be moments out on the court when they'd just stop playing and watch Michael Jordan," says fellow Lion Rob Sims. "We do that with Calvin. I've seen some amazing things..."

And from the mouth of Seattle Seahawks All-Pro cornerback Richard Sherman: "They tell you he's [6-foot-5] and runs a 4.3 [second] 40. Then you get out there, and he's faster than you think, quicker than you think. Taller and stronger than you think. . . Calvin's playing ball at a different level from anyone else."

JULIO JONES

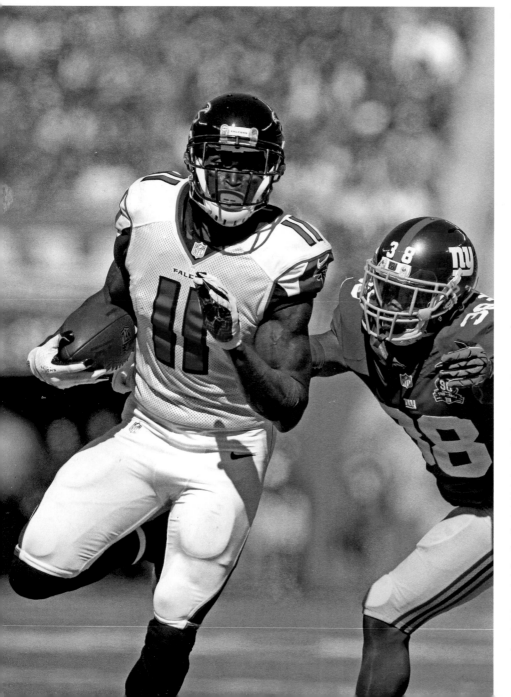

Quintorris Lopez Jones, better known as Julio, started pestering his mom, Queen Marvin, to let him play football when he was five. Concerned because he was smaller than the other kids in the rough-and-tumble Aaronville neighborhood of Foley, Alabama, she didn't let him on the field until he was 12.

"I'll tell you, he was out there playing one day, and he said, 'Mom, one day, when I get old enough, I'm going to play pro football, and I'm going to buy you a car and a new house,' " said Marvin. "I said, 'OK, I appreciate that.' "

It wasn't just the promised riches; Queen knew football would keep Julio out of trouble and give him an incentive to finish his homework. For the woman who made him come home before the streetlights came on, that mattered.

At Foley High School, Jones had 194 catches for 3,287 yards, 43 touchdowns, three rushing touchdowns, two kickoff and two punt return touchdowns, and two fumble returns for scores. As a senior he was named Alabama's Mr. Football and the Gatorade Player of the Year, and scouting services Rivals.com and Scout.com both named him the best high school receiver in the country.

Jones had his choice of schools, but he stayed close to home at the University of Alabama. In 40 games with the Crimson Tide, Jones caught

179 passes for 2,653 yards — both good for second in school history — with 15 touchdowns and 3,084 all-purpose yards. He was a two-time recipient of Alabama's Commitment to Academic Excellence Award, won the national title as a sophomore, and set school records in his junior year with 78 receptions and 1,133 yards before deciding it was time to take care of Queen.

The Atlanta Falcons had their sights set on Jones and were willing to pay a steep price to get him, sending five draft picks to the Cleveland Browns to move up to the sixth overall in the 2011 draft.

"I think the more they got to know him, the more they fell in love with him," says Nick Saban, the college coaching legend at Alabama, of the Falcons. "[It's because] of the kind of person he is, the kind of character he has and the kind of competitive character and toughness that he plays with."

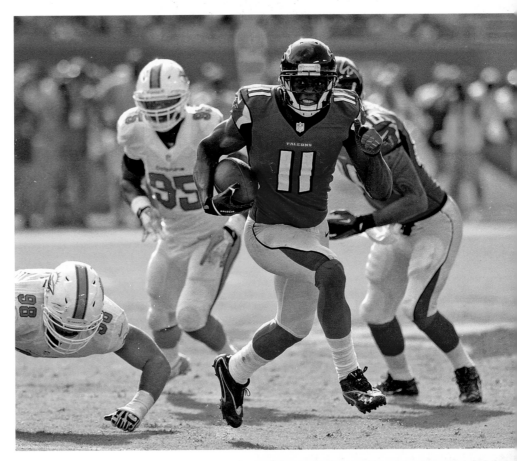

IN THE HUDDLE
Quintorris means "gladiator," and Jones has a tattoo of a football-playing gladiator, which covers his entire back.

The 2013 season demonstrated the value Jones brings to the Falcons. He was leading the league in receptions and yards heading into Week 5 of the season when he broke his foot — the same one he'd previously broken and had surgically repaired in 2011. Jones missed the rest of the season, and the Atlanta offense stalled. Without one of quarterback Matt Ryan's two favorite targets, the team's season was lost as the Falcons finished 4-12.

The Falcons' other main target is Roddy White, who had just posted an NFL-leading 115 receptions when the Falcons drafted Jones. Instead of White resenting the young phenom, he became his teacher, and Jones the eager student.

"I didn't come in and be like,

'I'm the number-one guy, I'm the number-one pick,'" says Jones. "I'm always willing to learn . . . I wouldn't be the person I am today without Roddy White. He's helped teach me how to be a man."

The bond grew deeper when White's brother was shot and killed in 2014. "Every day, he called me and checked up on me, asked me how I was doing; came down for the funeral; showed up at the house," says White of Jones. "You know, that was really, really special to me. I needed him to get through that."

Ten days later it was White's turn to provide support when Jones' older brother Phillip was shot and had to have his arm amputated.

Through it all, Jones, healthy again, had a career year in 2014. He set a career high (and franchise record) with 259 yards in Week 14 against the Green Bay Packers, the most the storied franchise had ever given up to one player. He injured his hip in the game, however, and missed the following week, which cost him a chance to end the season atop the

CAREER HIGHLIGHTS

- Two-time Pro Bowl selection (2012, 2014)

- NFL career leader in average receiving yards per game (88.4)

- Holds Atlanta franchise records for receiving yards in a game (259) and season (1,593)

league. Still, his 104 receptions and 1,593 yards for the season were both third in the NFL, and the latter set a new Falcons single-season high, breaking White's 2010 record.

For the five draft picks they parted with, the Falcons have had four seasons of Jones: 4,330 yards receiving, an average of 15.6 yards a catch and 88.4 yards a game — the highest yards per game in NFL history.

In return, Jones got a best friend and the money and security to take care of Queen.

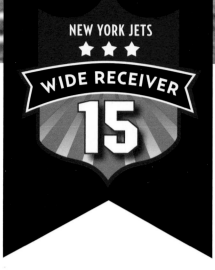

BRANDON MARSHALL

Freddie Marshall was a star quarterback in high school and a local Pittsburgh legend. He also spent time in jail on drug and domestic abuse charges. From an early age, his son Brandon Marshall witnessed violence and abuse close up; his was an unsettled upbringing in a gritty part of Steel City.

Hoping for a better life, in the fourth grade Brandon moved to Florida with his father and brother, while his mother and sister moved to Georgia.

As a senior at Lake Howell High School in Winter Park, Florida, Marshall had 1,056 yards receiving and 450 rushing, and he was state triple jump champion. His first choice was the University of Florida, but they wanted him to be a safety, so he went to the University of Central Florida, where he was featured on both sides of the ball. He had 112 receptions for 1,674 yards and 13 touchdowns, while also recording 52 tackles, an interception and a forced fumble in his seven starts as a safety.

In 2006, Marshall was drafted by the Denver Broncos in the 4th round, 119th overall. Later that year he caught his first NFL touchdown pass from Jay Cutler. The two players became fast friends and developed instant chemistry.

Off the field, Marshall was thrust into the role of breadwinner for his extended family, who expected support. Through it all, he had three straight seasons of over 100 catches and 1,100 yards for the Broncos.

In 2008, then Chiefs cornerback Brandon Flowers called Marshall "a defensive lineman playing wide receiver. He wants to inflict punishment on you. He wants you to try to tackle him so he can shove you off of him and get more yards."

IN THE HUDDLE
Marshall was the only player in the league with 1,000-plus yards receiving and the only with 80-plus receptions each season from 2007 through 2013. He also has two of the top-3 single-game reception totals in NFL history.

It was a statement about Marshall's prowess and his state of mind. The apple didn't fall far from the tree, and his troubled youth grew into a troubled adulthood. Marshall had several brushes with the law, including domestic violence charges, and Freddie was still around. When his son refused to give him money, he tried to run him over with his car.

In 2009, Marshall set an NFL record with 21 receptions in a single game, but he'd worn out his welcome in Denver and was traded to the Miami Dolphins in 2010. The Dolphins then made him the

highest-paid receiver in the league.

"I was a lost guy coming in," says Marshall of his early years in the NFL. "My second year in Miami is when there really was a transformation in my life and in my heart. I really started seeing the world the way it's supposed to be seen."

In 2011, Marshall and wife Michi renewed their Christian faith, and he announced that he suffers from borderline personality disorder, which is characterized by difficulty controlling emotions and impulses. It seemed his father passed down more than his football prowess, but his son wasn't going to simply accept the dark side of his genetics. Therapy taught him "to create boundaries and not walls. Boundaries protect; walls isolate."

After two years and another two seasons of over 1,000 yards receiving, Marshall was reunited with Cutler when he was traded to the Chicago Bears, where he finished second in the league with 118 receptions. His receptions and receiving yards (1,508) set Bears franchise records.

In 2013, Marshall tied an NFL record with his fifth season of 100 or more catches. He also donated $1 million from his contract with the Bears to mental health care, and in 2014 he and his wife started Project 375, a nonprofit organization dedicated to mental health awareness

and advocacy. The number 375 signifies the Pantone color code for lime green, the recognized color for mental health. Marshall ignored NFL rules and fines for going against league uniform codes and wore 375-colored cleats to start a conversation about the stigma of mental health.

The Bears were a miserable 5-11 in 2014, and Marshall and Cutler had public spats, which he likened to brothers fighting.

"We love each other, and we can also get into it, and it's always been that way and it will never change," says Marshall of Cutler. "I love him and his family, I love his sons, and I wish him the best."

Marshall was sent to New York

after the season, where the noted follower of fashion will be wearing Pantone 626 with the Jets. He's just the fourth NFL player in the last 20 years to be traded three or more times, and he still hasn't played in the postseason. It's been a long, strange trip, but Marshall is ready to settle down and find peace.

"I think [the Jets organization is] going to accept me for who I am and see that it's a personality — not a character — issue. So as we begin to build these relationships, you want to be able to be there for a while. Being a one-hit wonder or a rental definitely affects you emotionally. . .

I want to take this opportunity and make the best out of it."

GREEN BAY PACKERS
★ ★ ★

WIDE RECEIVER

87

JORDY NELSON

CAREER HIGHLIGHTS

- Pro Bowl selection (2014)
- Second Team All-Pro (2014)
- Holds the franchise single-season record with 1,519 yards receiving (2014)
- Consensus All-America selection (2007)

The little Manhattan that Jordy Nelson came to dominate as a university senior couldn't be more different from its counterpart in New York City. And those differences are personified by the Green Bay Packers wide receiver, whose quiet leadership and farm-bred work ethic speak volumes about the character he brings with him to Wisconsin.

Alan and Kim Nelson raised Jordy on the family cattle farm in northeast Kansas, where the family has farmed for generations. With hard labor and a little genetic help from the fast-twitch muscles he was blessed with, Nelson never met an athletic competition he didn't excel at.

At Riley County High School, Nelson was All-State in basketball as a senior and established school-career records for blocks, steals and assists, and he won state track titles in the 100-, 200- and 400-meter races and the long jump, setting division records in the 100- and 200-meter races.

But football was his sport, and he was Second Team All-State as both quarterback and defensive back. As a senior he threw for 1,029 yards and eight touchdowns, and rushed for 1,572 yards and 25 touchdowns.

From a small school in a small Kansas town, the only college interest came from Division II schools Emporia State and Washburn. Instead, Nelson chose to walk on at Kansas State — down the road in Manhattan — where the Nelsons had season tickets for the Wildcats. He was redshirted his first season and didn't see much of the field as a safety his second, but by the time he graduated he was a consensus All-American.

IN THE HUDDLE

Nelson had three touchdown catches of 80-plus yards from Week 16 of 2010 through Week 6 of 2011, the first player since the 1970 AFL-NFL merger with three 80-yard touchdown receptions over an eight-game span in the regular season.

In his sophomore year in 2005, Nelson switched to wide receiver and led the team in receptions, yards and receiving touchdowns. As a senior he set school records with 122 receptions for 1,606 yards, and he finished his career second in school history in both categories. He also ran back six punts, including 89- and 92-yard touchdown returns, and threw two passes in his senior year for two touchdowns.

The Green Bay Packers chose Nelson 36th overall with their first pick in the 2008 draft. Quiet on the field and off, Nelson's coming-out party was his nine catches for 140

yards in the Packers' 31–25 win over the Steelers in Super Bowl XLV following the 2010 season. His highlight reel from that game included a 29-yard touchdown reception to open the scoring. Teammates point to that game as the moment Nelson gained the confidence to become their best receiver and a locker-room leader.

The following season Nelson tied a Green Bay record with two touchdowns of 80 yards or more, and he scored in every single home game. His 15 touchdowns on the season were a career high and made him only the third player in Packers history to reach the mark.

Nelson has gone over 1,000 yards receiving in three of the past four seasons, falling short in 2012 when he missed four games with a hamstring injury that slowed him in the games he did play. In 2013 he led the league with 19 receptions of 25-plus yards,

the most by a Packer since the stat started being recorded in 1994. In 2014, Nelson had a career-high 98 receptions and was second in the NFL with 13 touchdown catches.

With a 15-yard pass from quarterback Aaron Rodgers in the fourth quarter of the final game of the 2014 season, Nelson broke a 19-year-old team record for single-season receiving yards and became the first player in the long and illustrious history of the team with over 1,500. He finished the year with 1,519 yards and earned long-overdue All-Pro and Pro Bowl honors.

Sports Illustrated called Nelson the "NFL's most dangerous deep threat" based on the former sprinter's speed, strength and smarts, as well as the chemistry he's developed with Rodgers. "Body language, unspoken adjustments, eye contact — we've made a lot of hay on those things,"

puns the passer.

And being from Manhattan, life in Green Bay — the NFL's smallest market — suits Nelson just fine. He returns home to help on the farm when he's not busy chewing up yards on NFL fields, and brings teammates along to show them the place that made him the player he is today.

"Farming teaches you that nothing is handed out," says Nelson. "If you take a day off, you have to work twice as hard the next day."

Nelson bought his own land back home and plans to retire there with wife Emily, whom he met in kindergarten, and their son, Royal. In the meantime he's helping his adopted state by filming ads for the Wisconsin Department of Tourism, which brought a 5.3 percent increase in visitor spending to the state in 2014. Next on Nelson's agenda is bringing back the Lombardi Trophy.

GREG OLSEN

It's not often an NFL general manager openly admits that he made a bad trade, but maybe it's easier to be candid when your mistake is so apparent.

Jerry Angelo was the Chicago Bears GM who drafted Greg Olsen with the second-last pick of the first round in 2007, and he's also the man who traded him to the Carolina Panthers for a third-round pick four years later.

"That's on me," confessed Angelo on a Chicago radio station of the fleecing by Carolina. "He's an excellent player, particularly in the passing game. He's [quarterback Cam] Newton's favorite target."

At 6-foot-5 and 253 pounds, Olsen is a big target, a large part of the Panthers' offense and a remarkably consistent performer.

It started at Wayne Hills High School in Wayne, New Jersey, where coach Chris Olsen won the first of his eight state titles in 2002 with his son on the roster as a senior. Greg was a USA Today First Team All-American that year.

The younger Olsen went on to the University of Miami, where he found himself among the nation's best young football players — and down the depth chart. With his football IQ and work ethic, he worked his way up, and in his junior year he led the Hurricanes with 40 catches and was a First Team All-ACC selection, before declaring for the 2007 draft.

IN THE HUDDLE

Olsen is the only tight end in the NFL with five or more receiving touchdowns every year since 2008.

In four years with the Bears, Olsen had 208 catches for 2,453 yards and 18 touchdowns; in four in Carolina he's had 257 receptions, 2,735 yards and 24 touchdowns. He's also played in 126 straight games and counting.

In 2012, Olsen set Carolina franchise records for the most single-season catches (69) and receiving yards (843) by a tight end, both of which were career highs. He then upped his reception record and led the Panthers with 73 in 2013, the first time since 1997 that a wide receiver did not lead the team in receptions or receiving yards. He broke his own record again

in 2014 with 84 catches, good for third in the NFL. His 1,008 receiving yards that season set a new team tight-end record and were second among NFL tight ends. Steady and reliable and taken for granted, he finally made the Pro Bowl for the first time.

"There are a lot of guys out there who are bigger names and who are recognized more," says Olsen. "I don't really care too much about that stuff. I feel very comfortable about what I bring to the team."

The Panthers are too. They signed Olsen to a three-year, $22.5 million contract extension before the 2015 season, with a $12 million signing bonus.

"We made it clear to them I wanted to finish my career here and wouldn't want to play anywhere else, and they kind of echoed that," says Olsen. He is also indebted to the organization for the help he and wife Kara received when son Trent Jerry "TJ" was born with hypoplastic left heart syndrome, which has led to four open heart surgeries. Trent's second name is for team owner Jerry Richardson.

Many nights Olsen slept at Levine Children's Hospital in Charlotte, where he and his wife set up The HEARTest Yard fund for kids like TJ, and coach Ron Rivera excused Olsen from practices to take care of TJ's twin, Talbot, and older brother, Tate, while Kara lived at the hospital.

"He's showing a lot of perseverance to endure so much," says Cam Newton. "It's beyond being a player. It's what type of man Greg Olsen really is, and he inspires a lot of people — on the field and off."

Cris Collinsworth, the former NFL receiver and TV analyst, agrees: "Playing football in the NFL is stressful enough. But to be able to balance his other duties as a husband and father so well really tells you all you need to know about Greg Olsen.

"I think ultimately that nobody is going to remember any of us for much of what we did on the football field. I think we are all going to be remembered and judged on what we do away from football, and Greg Olsen is getting it right. I admire him."

DENVER BRONCOS
★★★
WIDE RECEIVER
88

DEMARYIUS THOMAS

In what is becoming an annual rite of spring in Denver, a superstar was thrown under the bus. In this case it was Demaryius Thomas, who had just broken the Broncos' single-season record for receiving yards but was called out publicly for skipping voluntary off-season workouts.

The man doing the calling out is former Broncos quarterback and current team president John Elway, who can say and do as he pleases in the Mile High City because he brought two Super Bowl titles to town.

Entering the 2015 season, the Broncos applied the franchise tag to Thomas in order to keep him in Denver. The tag comes with a nice salary but not the long-term security he wants and has earned. He's Peyton Manning's top target, and he's made three straight Pro Bowls and been a Second Team All-Pro two years running.

It'll take a lot more than a public rebuke and financial power play to rattle Thomas, however. He's dealt with far worse.

When Thomas was 11, he and his mother, Katina Smith, lived in a trailer near Montrose, Georgia, population 154. The closest grocery store was a 40-minute drive away, and they had no car.

Grandmother Minnie Pearl Thomas was the matriarch, and her place is where Thomas stayed when his mother was at work. It is where the family ate Sunday dinner after church. It was also where she sold crack cocaine.

In 1999, Demaryius' mother and grandmother were arrested on drug charges after a police raid on his home — where the drugs were stashed — in the middle of the night. His mom was sentenced to 24 years in prison, and his grandmother got two life terms. In the wake of the arrests, it was the police who took Demaryius to the school bus. That surreal trip is still his defining moment. It was "the worst bus ride of anyone's life," recalls Thomas.

CAREER HIGHLIGHTS

- Two-time Second Team All-Pro selection (2013–14)

- Three-time Pro Bowl selection (2012–14)

- Holds the franchise records for receiving yards in a game (226) and a season (1,619)

- Holds the Super Bowl single-game record with 13 catches (XLVIII)

As the trial approached, Katina was urged to testify against her mother to get a reduced sentence, but even with her mother's urging, she refused. For a couple years Thomas floated between relatives' homes, until he found a permanent place with Aunt Shirley and Uncle James — the latter a disciplinarian who taught his nephew responsibility. Demaryius had a curfew and had to get up at 5:30 a.m. on weekends to pick fields of peas. At West Laurens High School, good grades were the priority, but Thomas was also an All-State receiver and played on the state champion basketball team.

IN THE HUDDLE

Thomas is the only receiver in the NFL to have at least 90 catches, 1,400 yards and 10 touchdowns in each of the last three seasons.

Thomas went to Georgia Tech, where he ranked fourth in school history in receiving yards and touchdown catches. As a senior he was second in the country and first in school history with a 25.1 yards-per-catch average, with 46 receptions and 1,154 yards. He also started to let his mother back into his life after refusing to see her in high school. After a road game at Florida State in his junior year, just five miles from her prison, he visited her for the first time in five years.

The Broncos selected Thomas 22nd overall in 2010, and he came to national attention in the 2011 playoffs. In the AFC wild-card game, he had four receptions for 204 yards, the most in Broncos playoff history and the second-highest receiving average (51.0) in a single game in NFL history. The exclamation mark was his 80-yard touchdown reception on the first play of overtime for a 29–23 shocker over the Pittsburgh Steelers, the longest overtime scoring play in NFL postseason history and the high point of quarterback Tim Tebow's fame and short career.

Elway jettisoned Tebow and brought in Manning in the off-season, and Thomas caught Manning's first touchdown pass as a Bronco. Thomas had more than 1,400 yards in each of their first two seasons together, and had a knack for big receptions. He had the only Broncos touchdown in Super Bowl XLVIII, and his 13 receptions set a championship game record, the lone bright spot in a 43–8 shellacking by the Seattle Seahawks.

During the 2014 season, Thomas caught Manning's 509th career touchdown pass, which broke the all-time QB record. Thomas shone all season, playing ten games with 100-plus yards, including a team-record 226 yards against the Arizona Cardinals. He snagged 111 receptions, and set a Broncos record with 1,619 yards. Both marks were good for second in the league.

No matter where his new contract comes from, Thomas will be rewarded as one of the best in the world at catching footballs, and he knows where the money is going. He envisions buying land in Georgia and building several houses for the family, including one for his mother, who is nearing the end of her prison sentence.

Thomas says of his plan, "I'm making it my responsibility to give her a soft place to land."

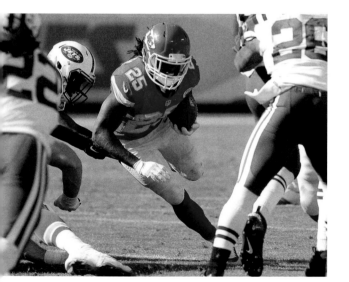

RUNNING BACKS

PITTSBURGH STEELERS
★ ★ ★
RUNNING BACK
26

Le'VEON BELL

"My mother was my first and strongest offensive line," wrote Pittsburgh Steelers running back Le'Veon Bell on Medium.com, expressing his gratitude for Thanksgiving 2014. "Raising my two brothers and me as a single working mom, her résumé is far more remarkable than any 200-yard game on mine."

Born in Columbus, Ohio, Bell didn't have much growing up, but his mother, Lisa, never let him feel disadvantaged. She made sure that they lived in neighborhoods that allowed him to go to the right schools and that he had all the opportunities and resources he needed to succeed.

At Groveport Madison High School in Ohio, Le'Veon Bell was rated a mere two-star prospect by analysts. College interest was equally lukewarm, and Bell was mulling offers from Bowling Green, Eastern Michigan and Marshall. But his principal, whose father coached Michigan State University coach Mark Dantonio in high school, urged the Spartans to have a look. They came calling when they lost three running backs and a prized recruit.

"He didn't run with the same kind of passion, drive you see now. He was a dime a dozen. I can honestly say I didn't anticipate this," said Josh Helmholdt, Midwest

recruiting analyst for Rivals.com, when Bell emerged as one of the country's best runners at MSU.

As a junior in 2012, Bell carried much of the MSU offense. He led the nation with 382 carries, was the first Spartan to lead the Big Ten in rushing since 1990, and had 32 receptions and 13 touchdowns (12 rushing, 1 receiving). His 1,793 yards rushing were the second most in MSU history, and he was first in the country in yards after contact, with 922. In the last game of the season, he played through a shoulder injury and had the best game of his collegiate career, with 266 yards on 35 carries.

Going out on a high note, Bell left school a year early and declared for the 2013 draft. At the NFL scouting combine, he ran a pedestrian 4.6 seconds in the 40-yard dash — 15th fastest among running backs — but he finished third in the three-cone drill. Bell's running is based less on raw speed than on cutting and making people miss, and Pittsburgh coach Mike Tomlin told Bell if he lost some weight he'd be successful.

Two months later, Tomlin and the Steelers chose Bell in the second round, 48th overall, and his NFL career got off to an inauspicious start. He missed three preseason games and the first three games of the regular season because of foot and ankle injuries. But Bell hit his stride in the latter part of the season, and with

1,259 yards from scrimmage in just 13 games played, he passed Franco Harris for the most yards from scrimmage by a Steelers rookie.

After slimming down in the off-season to become quicker, Bell found a new gear in 2014. He led the AFC with 1,361 yards, averaging 4.7 yards per carry, and had eight touchdowns. He was First Team All-Pro and second in the NFL in just about everything else — rushing yards, yards from scrimmage, all-purpose yards and touches.

IN THE HUDDLE

In 2014, Bell became the second player in NFL history, after Marshall Faulk, to have 1,350-plus rushing yards and 850-plus receiving yards in a single season, and became the third player, after Faulk and Barry Sanders, to have more than 2,000 yards from scrimmage in a season without fumbling.

The linemen opening holes for Bell called him "Walter Junior" after he joined Walter Payton as the only other running back in NFL history to have 200 yards from scrimmage in three straight games. The entire squad voted Bell the team's most valuable player at season's end.

"The things that he did this year in more than just the running game — the passing game, catching the ball, blocking — when you think of an MVP, he is a guy that should come to mind," said quarterback Ben Roethlisberger.

The Steelers were missing their MVP after Bell hyperextended his knee in the last game of the regular season and missed the wild-card game against the rival Baltimore Ravens, which the Steelers lost 30–17. And Pittsburgh will be without him to start the 2015 season too.

Bell and then-teammate LeGarrette Blount were pulled over by the police during the 2014 preseason, and Bell was charged with DUI and marijuana possession. He

reached a plea deal for 15 months' probation, and the NFL suspended him for the first three games of the 2015 season.

"I'm building something wonderful in Pittsburgh, but I know that nothing can be built without a solid foundation, without the right materials," said Bell in the Medium.com essay. "For me, that all starts with my mother and her unwavering belief that despite life's twists and turns, its highs and lows, it's important to maintain balance and perspective."

Lisa taught Le'Veon that he's only as good as his word. Now it's time for him to heed hers.

CAREER HIGHLIGHTS

- First Team All-Pro (2014)
- Pro Bowl selection (2014)
- Holds Steelers franchise records with 2,215 yards from scrimmage, and receptions (83) and receiving yards (854) by a running back
- Most Improved Player as voted by the Pro Football Writers of America (2014)

JAMAAL CHARLES

Growing up in Port Arthur, Texas, Jamaal Charles took special education because of a serious learning disability. The oil town was tough — with the temptations of gangs and drugs — but the strong women in Jamaal's life believed in him. And he could run like the wind.

A trio of women raised Jamaal, including his single mom, Sharon, grandmother Mazelle Smith Miller, and his aunt Arlene LeBlanc. Together, they kept Jamaal in school and in sports — his grandmother provided the rooting (until she lost her battle with cancer when Jamaal was eight), and his aunt

helped with his studies. He struggled academically, but was a blur on the field, winning a bronze medal in the 400-meter hurdles at the 2003 World Youth Championships, and rushing for 4,107 yards and 50 touchdowns in his junior and senior seasons at Memorial High School.

The University of Texas had doubts about his ability to handle classes, but he persevered, helping the Longhorns win the 2005 national title as a freshman; he also became a Big 12 Second Team All-Academic.

Skipping his senior season, Charles was expected to be a late first-rounder in the 2008

draft after his 18 touchdown junior season. But questions in his scouting report about his strength and toughness caused him to fall to the third round, where the Kansas City Chiefs selected him 73rd overall. As he waited for his name to be called, he cried privately.

It wasn't until the team released veteran Larry Johnson late in Charles' second NFL season (2009) that he had a chance to prove himself. He picked up the gauntlet and ran with it — for over a hundred yards in each of the final four games, punctuated with a team-record 259 yards in the season finale.

CAREER HIGHLIGHTS

- Two-time First Team All-Pro selection (2010, 2013)
- Second Team All-Pro (2012)
- Four-time Pro Bowl selection (2010, 2012–14)
- The NFL's all-time leader in yards per carry average (5.49 at the end of 2014)
- Led the NFL in total touchdowns (19) and tied for first in rushing touchdowns (12) in 2013

The following season Charles was a First Team All-Pro and was named to the Pro Bowl after rushing for 1,467 yards and an astounding 6.4 yards per carry, but it wasn't a smooth run into the record books from there. In 2011 he tore his ACL, a potentially career-ending injury. But the physical can be fixed; emotional scars take much longer to heal.

On December 1, 2012, teammate Jovan Belcher killed his girlfriend, Kasandra Perkins, and then shot himself at the Chiefs' stadium. Perkins was the cousin of Charles' wife, Whitney, and the guilt over having to leave Whitney that night to prepare for the next day's game — and for introducing Perkins to Belcher — started to eat him.

IN THE HUDDLE
In 2013 against the Oakland Raiders, Charles became the first player in NFL history to have four receiving touchdowns and one rushing touchdown in the same game.

Charles dedicated the game to Perkins, running for 127 yards in a win over the Carolina Panthers and then broke down in the locker room afterwards. In the aftermath he turned to his aunt for emotional and spiritual support, while trying his best to be strong for Whitney and their two daughters, Makaila and Makenzie.

The quiet superstar withdrew from the public eye even further, throwing himself into new coach Andy Reid's system in 2013. Charles' talent was fully realized under Reid as he led the NFL in touchdowns (19), thanks to career highs on the ground (12) and through the air (7).

Playing through injuries — including a high ankle sprain — in 2014, Charles made history and joined immortal company. With 1,033

yards rushing and 5.0 yards per carry, he became the third player in history, after Hall of Famers Jim Brown and Barry Sanders, to have at least five seasons of 1,000 yards and a 5.0-yard average. No other active player has done it more than twice, and Emmitt Smith and Walter Payton, the two leading rushers in NFL history, managed the feat once apiece.

Over the 2013 and 2014 seasons, Charles' 33 combined touchdowns (21 rushing, 12 receiving) led all NFL players, and he's currently the NFL's all-time leader in rushing average among running backs with at least 1,000 carries. At 5.49 yards per carry, he ranks ahead of Brown (5.22),

Sanders (4.99) and Adrian Peterson (4.96).

Far from the bright lights and temptations of NFL riches, Charles still returns to his grandmother's old house in Port Arthur in the offseason, where he runs a football camp for the next generation. He also awards scholarships to Texas students with learning disabilities.

"One thing I took from my grandma when she passed away was that she was always like a guardian for everyone," Charles said. "She inspired a lot of people with the way she carried herself. The only thing I can go by is how I inspire people by the way I play. I wanted to inspire little kids to look at me and do [things] the right way."

MATT FORTE

CAREER HIGHLIGHTS

- Two-time Pro Bowl selection (2011, 2013)
- Set the NFL record for receptions by a running back (102) in 2014
- Set franchise rookie records for rushing yards (1,238) and yards from scrimmage (1,715) in 2008

When Matt Forte was seven years old, he decided he wanted to be an NFL player. His father, Gene, sat him down and explained, "There are only 2,000 people in the United States who are going to play professional football every year."

Matt replied, "I'm going to be one of those 2,000."

Gene, more than most parents, knew what it took to become an NFL player. In 1977 he was captain of the Tulane University football team, and though he received offers to attend NFL training camps, he chose to take a job at Shell and settle down in Slidell, Louisiana, with his wife, Gilda, instead.

Growing up, Matt enrolled in soccer, baseball, basketball, gymnastics, karate and swimming. His dad tried to dissuade him from playing football, because knee surgery in college was one of the reasons his own career was cut short and he didn't attend the NFL camps.

Matt couldn't be kept off the field though, and he dominated on the gridiron at Slidell High School, where he was district MVP and Second Team All-State before following his dad's footsteps to Tulane. It was one of only two schools to offer him a scholarship, and Forte arrived low on Tulane's depth chart. But with his football intelligence and work ethic, he quickly climbed the ladder.

Forte had his own knee problems in college. He tore his posterior cruciate ligament and missed half his junior year, but came back and rushed for 2,127 yards (the seventh highest in NCAA history), scored 23 touchdowns and was named MVP of the Senior Bowl.

In 2008, the Chicago Bears picked Forte in the second round, 44th overall, and his legend was born before the season began. He arrived at minicamp in his first bespoke suit while his new teammates all showed up in the customary sweats.

"Matt is an unusual guy, and I don't mean unusual as in weird or strange," says Jerry Angelo, the former Bears general manager who drafted Forte. "Even though he's quiet, he has a lot of confidence in himself. [Wearing] a suit to minicamp, he was saying, 'I'm here for business. I'm a professional.'"

Forte's play lived up to his style. His fourth career carry was a 50-yard touchdown run, and he set the franchise rookie records for rushing yards (1,238) and yards from scrimmage

(1,715) in a season. Those marks broke Gale Sayers' records, and Forte also led the team with 63 receptions — a team record for running backs.

In his second season with the Bears, Forte sprained his MCL, which robbed him of his speed and his first step. He kept the injury a secret, however, and didn't miss any playing time.

A healthy Forte bounced back in 2010, rushing for 1,069 yards and gaining a total of 1,616 all-purpose yards and nine touchdowns. In 2011 he was well on his way to a career season when he went down in the 12th game of the year with a Grade II (partial tear) MCL sprain. At that point he was leading the league with 1,487 total yards, was just three shy of 1,000 rushing yards, and he'd accounted for 38 percent of the Bears' total yardage. He ran for 205 yards against the Carolina Panthers, becoming the third Bears running back to break

200 yards in a game (following Hall of Famers Sayers and Walter Payton), and he was on pace to break two single-season team records: Payton's rushing mark and Sayers' all-purpose yards.

IN THE HUDDLE
Forte was the first player in NFL history to have 900-plus rushing yards and 400-plus receiving yards in each of his first four seasons, and the only player in Bears history to have 1,000-plus rushing and 500-plus receiving in multiple seasons, which he's done three times (2010, 2013, 2014).

Forte has missed only five games in seven seasons, and none in the past two years. His commitment to fitness, healthy living and preventive maintenance is legendary. And he's an elusive runner, avoiding traumatic hits as much as a featured running back can. He'll turn 30 during the 2015 season, but he's shown no signs of slowing down. In 2013 he had

career highs with 1,339 rushing yards and 1,933 total yards, and in 2014 he ran for 1,038 yards and had 1,846 total. In both seasons he was third in the NFL in yards from scrimmage, and since he joined the league in 2008, no player has gained more than his 11,431 yards.

In 2014, *Sports Illustrated* called Forte "more important to his team than any other back in the NFL," and that was before he set a new single-season NFL record for running backs, with 102 receptions.

"He's a pro, man," said Bears second-year guard Kyle Long after Forte broke the record. "People who have been around football . . . [know] that Matt is the ultimate pro. They know what that entails. And Matt is all about that."

And it's not just the young players who admire Forte. "He's the same year as me, but he's the veteran I emulate," admits tight end Martellus Bennett.

ARIAN FOSTER

"In a nutshell, the Fosters — we don't think inside the box," says patriarch Carl, and a case in point is his son's name, Arian. The name is an abbreviated version of Aquarians, meaning "holder of knowledge" — the quest for which is also a family trait.

Half Mexican-American and half African-American, Arian Foster endured racial taunts and struggled with his identity while growing up in New Mexico and California. To escape, he ran the dunes with his father at Pacific Beach in San Diego. This early training led to a stellar high school career and a scholarship to the University of Tennessee.

"When you put in that kind of time and effort, there is a spiritual aspect that has to take place inside of you as an athlete," says Carl. "I watched him grow in his demeanor and responsibility. He had an attitude that he wasn't going to quit."

At Tennessee, Foster was a philosophy major who studied Hindu teachings, poetry and yoga while rushing for 1,231 yards on a 10-4 team as a junior. In his senior season he had to share the carries, leading the team in rushing but with only 597 yards, and the Volunteers sputtered to a 5-7 record. These results got coach Phillip Fulmer fired and sent

Foster's stock plummeting.

After going undrafted, the Houston Texans signed Foster as a free agent in 2009, released him and then signed him to the practice squad. He was elevated to the active roster midway through the season, and in six games he averaged a modest 42.8 yards per game, which was not a portent for 2010.

Foster got his shot as a starter against the Indianapolis Colts in the first game of 2010, and he didn't waste the opportunity. He ran for the seventh-highest total in league history: a franchise-

record 231 yards, and he scored three touchdowns on 33 carries. By season's end Foster led the NFL in rushing yards (1,616), yards from scrimmage (2,220), scoring by a non-kicker (108 points), touchdowns (18) and first downs (123), all of which were franchise records.

In 2011, Foster missed three games with a hamstring injury, but he still rushed for 1,224 yards. The Texans were an injury-stung team, with key players missing significant time. Despite the loss of manpower, Houston won the AFC South as well as the first playoff game in franchise history. That was a 31–10 victory over the Cincinnati Bengals, in which Foster accounted for 54 percent of Houston's offense. The win set up a showdown with the Baltimore Ravens and their vaunted defense. Foster shredded the Ravens for 132 yards and a touchdown, becoming the first player to gain 100 yards against Baltimore all season, and the first ever in the playoffs. But it somehow wasn't enough, and the Ravens prevailed 20–13.

Picking up where he left off, Foster led the league in 2012 with 15 rushing and 17 total touchdowns, and gained 1,424 yards on the ground. He was a force in the playoffs too, torching the Bengals for 140 yards and a touchdown in a 19–13 AFC wild-card win. His three consecutive 100-plus yard playoff performances set an NFL record.

IN THE HUDDLE

Foster led the NFL in rushing in 2010 with the most yards ever gained by an undrafted player, surpassing by one yard Priest Holmes' record of 1,615 set in 2002.

The life span of a running back is notoriously short, and when Foster went down with a back injury in Week 9 of the 2013 season, few thought he'd recover to be the dominant runner he had been.

But his father's lessons from the dunes and his open-minded worldview were allies in his rehab, and 2014 saw Foster rush for the third-most yards of his career (1,246), tying his second-best season in yards per carry (4.8) and going to his fourth Pro Bowl. He also diversified, setting a new career high with five touchdown catches to go with eight on the ground.

"As soon as you get into the NFL, they're always going to tell you what you can't do," says Foster, who will be 29 when the 2015 season begins. "One of them is being a 30-year-old running back. [There are] always outliers. I believe myself to be an outlier."

And he's now the one imparting wisdom to the next generation. In an open letter penned to daughter Zeniah, he wrote, "No one is any better than you are, and you are no better than anyone else. We are all doing the best we can to figure out this thing we call life . . . I've learned things from a man with a PhD, a man who lived under a bridge and a child. Treat everyone with kindness. It goes a long way."

CAREER HIGHLIGHTS

- First Team All-Pro (2010)
- Second Team All-Pro (2011)
- Four-time Pro Bowl selection (2010–12, 2014)
- Led the NFL in rushing yards (1,616), rushing touchdowns (16) and total touchdowns (18) in 2010

MARSHAWN LYNCH

CAREER HIGHLIGHTS

- First Team All-Pro (2012)
- Second Team All-Pro (2014)
- Five-time Pro Bowl selection (2008, 2011–14)
- Tied for the NFL lead in rushing touchdowns in 2013 (12) and 2014 (13)
- Led the NFL in total touchdowns in 2014 with 17 (13 rushing, 4 receiving)

On January 8, 2011, there was a minor earthquake in downtown Seattle. The ground below CenturyLink Field (then known as Qwest Field) seemed to be moving, yet there was no tectonic activity in the region. The source was the Seahawks' Marshawn Lynch rumbling downfield in his first career playoff game.

Lynch's 67-yard touchdown run in the fourth quarter, during which he broke eight tackles, was the winning score as the Seahawks shocked the defending Super Bowl champion New Orleans Saints 41–36. The crowd's reaction was so intense it registered on the Richter scale.

Having grown up in the Bay Area, Lynch is no stranger to earthquakes or to frenzied football fans. In his senior year at Oakland Technical High School, he ran for 1,722 yards and 23 touchdowns in only eight games. At the University of California, Berkeley, he won the Pac-10 Offensive Player of the Year award.

Forgoing his final year of college, Lynch was drafted by the Buffalo Bills with the 12th overall pick in 2007. The move to a colder climate didn't faze him. Lynch became the first

Bills rookie since Greg Bell in 1984 to run for over 1,000 yards, but off-field issues halted the momentum.

Lynch was arrested on drug and weapons charges three days after his appearance in the 2008 Pro Bowl. He escaped jail time but not the long arm of the NFL's personal conduct policy, which Commissioner Roger Goodell cited to suspend Lynch for the first three games of the 2009 season. The emergence of Fred Jackson in Buffalo spelled the end for Lynch in New York State, and the troubled running back was moved to Seattle in 2010.

IN THE HUDDLE

According to Pro Football Focus, in 2014 Lynch led the league with 101 missed tackles. He was also first among running backs with a 94.3 elusive rating (a combination of missed tackles forced, touches, and yards after contact averages).

In the Pacific Northwest, Lynch brought "Beast Mode" — a ferocious, unstoppable running style — and Skittles to the attention of the football world. After one stirring touchdown in 2011, a camera caught a trainer giving Skittles to Lynch,

a tradition dating back to when his mother rewarded him after scoring. Skittles offered Lynch a two-year supply and a custom dispenser for his locker.

If Lynch drew the spotlight to the Emerald City, winning kept it there. Drafting quarterback Russell Wilson in 2012 and the emergence of the "Legion of Boom" defense made the Seahawks a force — one with swagger and personality.

In 2012, Lynch set career highs in yards (1,590), yards per game (5.0), 100-yard games (10) and total yards from scrimmage (1,786), to go with 12 touchdowns. He upped his touchdown total to 14 in 2013 and set a Seahawks postseason record with 140 rushing yards against the Saints in the 2013 NFC Divisional game. Seattle romped through the remainder of the postseason, finishing with a 43–8 decimation of Peyton Manning and the Denver Broncos in Super Bowl XLVIII.

In 2014, Lynch had an NFL-best 17 total touchdowns, but the playoffs that year will be remembered for the one he didn't get a chance to score.

In the NFC Championship against the Green Bay Packers, Lynch ran for 157 yards to help the Seahawks advance to back-to-back Super Bowls, which set up one of the more memorable media-day sound bites. Fined $100,000 earlier in the season for his refusal to speak to the media, he simply repeated the sentence "I'm just here so I don't get fined" 25 times to avoid another $500,000 penalty.

That mini-drama faded quickly once the Super Bowl started. Down 28–24 with less than a minute to play, the Seahawks were on the New England Patriots' 5-yard line after a circus catch by Jermaine Kearse put the momentum and fate in Seattle's hands. Lynch eclipsed 100 yards with a 4-yard carry to put the ball on the 1, but with the best power runner in the NFL a virtual lock to score, Seattle coach Pete Carroll called for a pass. It was intercepted on the goal line, and the Patriots won their first title in a decade. Said Cris Collinsworth on NBC, "I'm sitting here, and I absolutely cannot believe that play call. If I lose the Super Bowl because Marshawn Lynch can't get it in from the 1-yard line, so be it. So be it. But there is no way — I just don't believe the call."

Immediately after the game, Lynch answered one question about it, simply saying, "This is a team game." Away from American media a month later, he opened up a bit more.

In Turkey for an American Football Without Barriers camp, Lynch was interviewed on a national sports network. "To be honest with you, I would be lying if I didn't tell you that I was expecting the ball. Yes, I was expecting the ball.

But in life these things happen."

Maybe it's the wisdom that comes with age or the groundswell of support after the Super Bowl, but the Beast was at peace.

LeSEAN McCOY

LeSean McCoy was given the nickname Shady by his mom, Daphne, when he was a toddler because of the way his moods swung. It was also a pretty cool handle for the boy who quickly became a football legend in Harrisburg, Pennsylvania.

"Each year, I'd go back and watch him play midgets, and I'd say, 'I can't wait until I get him,'" says Bishop McDevitt High School coach Jeff Weachter. "He had so much natural ability."

McCoy didn't disappoint. He was twice named to the

Pennsylvania Class 4A All-State First Team, running for 5,389 yards and 59 touchdowns over the two seasons, and won Player of the Year as a junior. He was one of the most sought-after players in the country, but in his senior year he suffered a compound fracture of the right ankle, and the interest of several top colleges waned. McCoy became depressed, and his grades dropped. On the advice of older brother LeRon and a suggestion from one of the college coaches, he transferred to Milford Academy in New Berlin, New York, to focus on rehab and academics.

"He was homesick way out there," said Aaron Berry, a teammate at McDevitt and in college. "He's a very social person. And there wasn't anything out there but a Walmart."

Loneliness made McCoy change his mind and path, deciding to attend the closer-to-home University of Pittsburgh instead of Miami. In two seasons McCoy rushed for more than 2,800 yards and with 36 touchdowns, breaking the NCAA record for touchdowns as a freshman and a sophomore, which had been held by former Panther Larry Fitzgerald of the Arizona Cardinals.

McCoy got to stay in Pennsylvania when the Philadelphia Eagles took him in the second round of the 2009 draft, and in his first year in the NFL, he set an Eagles

rookie record with 637 rushing yards. In 2010, McCoy took a stranglehold on the starting running back job and helped the Eagles finish third in the NFL in points, second in total offense and first in plays of 20 yards or more. He set an Eagles record with a 5.2-yard rushing average and was the only player to lead his team in both rushing and receiving. He wasn't named an All-Pro that year, but he did make the All-Joe Team, an annual award given by USA TODAY to underappreciated overachievers.

IN THE HUDDLE

In 2011, McCoy became the first Eagle to lead the NFL in rushing touchdowns and total touchdowns since Steve Van Buren in 1947, and he broke a Van Buren record by scoring in nine straight games.

If McCoy didn't quite get the credit he deserved in 2010, he forced people to sit up and take notice in 2011. He set an Eagles record by scoring a touchdown in nine straight games and led the NFL in first downs (102), 10-plus yard rushes (48), rushing touchdowns (17) and total touchdowns (20). He was a First Team All-Pro and Pro Bowl selection, but an ankle injury in Week 16 cost him a shot at the rushing title.

McCoy became the Eagles' all-time leading rusher in 2014, with a franchise total of 6,792 yards, on the back of strong seasons in 2013 and 2014, which followed an injury-shortened 2012. But his resurgence and career marks weren't enough to keep him in Philadelphia. One year after cutting the Eagles' best receiver, DeSean Jackson, second-year coach Chip Kelly swapped McCoy to Buffalo for linebacker Kiko Alonso. It was a trade that shocked the NFL and fueled rumors that Kelly didn't like McCoy's shifty running style. With the extra salary cap space, the Eagles signed free agent DeMarco Murray, the NFL's leading rusher in 2014 and the only running back to have more yards than McCoy over the past two seasons — by 40 yards.

"I made the mistake of thinking that I had arrived," says brother LeRon, who suffered an injury after his one season as an Arizona Cardinals receiver and never played again. "And so that's my big thing with LeSean — never think that you have arrived."

McCoy, who will be 27 in the 2015 season, is still in his prime, and the former candy addict is now a nutrition and fitness convert. Experience has also taught him how to avoid big hits, which will help him survive in an offense without a marquee quarterback. And further, new coach Rex Ryan is a lover of the ground game.

A new five-year, $40 million contract showed the Bills' commitment to McCoy. While he wasn't crazy about leaving Pennsylvania for New York State again, McCoy's warming to Buffalo and his new team.

"Money wasn't the first reason to make me want to come here," says McCoy. "Even when I knew [about the contract offer], I was like, 'I'm not going there… and then I realized it was the best for me. This is a team that wants me. Coach Ryan is a winner and he wants to run the ball."

CAREER HIGHLIGHTS

- Two-time First Team All-Pro selection (2011, 2013)

- Three-time Pro Bowl selection (2011, 2013–14)

- Led the NFL in rushing (1,607 yards), rushing yards per game (100.4), yards from scrimmage (2,146) and touches (366) in 2013

- Led the NFL in first downs (102), 10-plus yard rushes (48), rushing touchdowns (17) and total touchdowns (20) in 2011

- Eagles all-time leading rusher (6,792 yards)

DeMARCO MURRAY

DeMarco Murray is extremely reluctant to talk about himself. Growing up outside Las Vegas, Nevada, with three brothers and three sisters, he may not have had the chance. When he did try, he was put in his place.

"His older brothers were always challenging him," says his father, Kevin.

At Bishop Gorman High School, Murray was All-State as a senior, running for 1,947 yards and 27 touchdowns. He added seven more receiving touchdowns, while also recording 64 tackles, three sacks and two interceptions as a defensive back. But it was

his basketball props that may have made the ultimate difference in his getting a football scholarship.

In front of Oklahoma football coach Bob Stoops, Murray, who was also on the state-winning basketball team, was encouraged to dunk a basketball by his Bishop Gorman football coach.

"I was thinking a normal dunk," said coach David White about the 360-degree windmill jam Murray unleashed. "And then DeMarco started that one, and I thought, 'What if he misses and falls flat on his face?' When I asked him about it later, he said missing never crossed his mind."

Murray didn't miss when he got to Oklahoma either. After a redshirt freshmen season, he set a school record in his very first game with five touchdowns. By the end of his four years as a Sooner, he set records for career all-purpose yards (6,718), touchdowns (65), total points (390), and receiving yards by a running back (1,571), despite a dislocated kneecap in 2007 and ruptured hamstring in 2008.

IN THE HUDDLE

In 2014, Murray set an NFL record by rushing for over 100 yards in each of the first eight games of the season, breaking Jim Brown's record of six in 1958, and he became just the seventh player since 1960 with at least 12 100-yard games in a season, tied for second most in history.

As the 2011 draft unfolded, Murray remained unpicked, with some thinking he was injury-prone. Dallas Cowboys owner Jerry Jones got a call from former Oklahoma and Dallas coach Barry Switzer.

"This kid is a first-round talent falling into your lap, and if you don't take him, you're as crazy as that time you didn't take Randy Moss," said Switzer.

The Cowboys drafted Murray 71st overall, and he set a Cowboys single-game record in his first year by rushing for 253 yards against the St. Louis Rams. The total was the second most by a rookie in NFL history, and included a 91-yard touchdown run — the longest first career

touchdown run since the AFL-NFL merger in 1970. But 2011 was a shortened season because of a broken ankle, and a foot injury cost Murray six games in the middle of the 2012 season.

In 2013, Murray made the Pro Bowl for the first time after rushing for 1,121 yards and nine touchdowns. But it was in 2014 that the Cowboys' offensive line emerged as the NFL's most dominant. That paved the way for a record-smashing year for Murray, in which he broke Hall of Famer Jim Brown's record of consecutive 100-yard rushing games by accomplishing the feat in eight straight contests. He also eclipsed the 1,000-yard barrier in the eighth game, setting a franchise record and reaching the mark faster than all but four players in NFL history.

Murray led the NFL in rushing that season, and it wasn't even close — his 1,845 yards were 484 more than second-leading rusher Le'Veon Bell of the Pittsburgh Steelers. The Dallas runner was also first in the league in yards from scrimmage with 2,261, and tied for the league lead with 13 rushing touchdowns. And he played the last two games with a metal plate in his left hand and a hard plastic shell on it to protect a repaired metacarpal bone.

"Just unbelievable courage and toughness and pride," said Cowboys tight end Jason Witten. "Seeing that gains a lot of respect. He's all about the team."

But up against the salary cap, the Cowboys let Murray hit the free-agent market, and the Philadelphia Eagles signed him to a five-year contract. It was the first time since 1947 that the reigning rushing champion changed teams.

In the City of Brotherly Love with Dallas' NFC East rival, Murray will have plenty of chances to prove the Cowboys made a mistake. He was quietly motivated when five other running backs were drafted ahead of him in 2011. Now that he's done proving his draft position was unwarranted, he lets his play do the talking when asked about Dallas' decision.

"You can't outrun everyone; you can't make everyone miss. So sometimes you've gotta try to impose your will on the opposition."

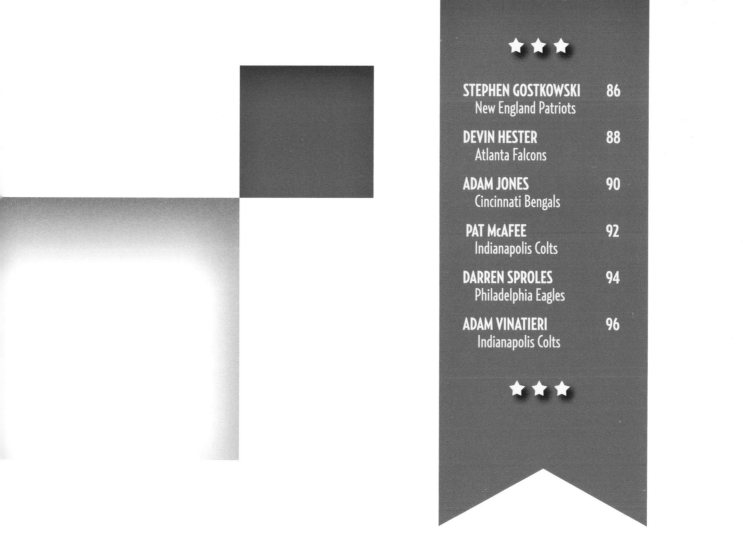

STEPHEN GOSTKOWSKI	86
New England Patriots	
DEVIN HESTER	88
Atlanta Falcons	
ADAM JONES	90
Cincinnati Bengals	
PAT McAFEE	92
Indianapolis Colts	
DARREN SPROLES	94
Philadelphia Eagles	
ADAM VINATIERI	96
Indianapolis Colts	

SPECIAL TEAMS

STEPHEN GOSTKOWSKI

Stephen Carroll Gostkowski lettered in football, soccer and baseball at Madison Central High in Mississippi, earning All-State honors in each sport. But it was baseball that paved his way to the NFL.

Gostkowski admits the pressure of recruiting got to him during his senior football season, and he was benched as a result of his poor play. His nerves cost him the scholarships he'd been offered. But on the diamond he was unaffected, pitching to an 8-2 record and a 1.40 earned run average that year — good enough to be signed by the University of Memphis.

Convinced by his parents to try out for the football team anyway, Gostkowski was a walk-on who earned a scholarship and the starting kicker job before the season began.

When asked in college which sport he'd choose if he had to, Gostkowski leaned towards baseball. "There is so much more pressure kicking field goals. You could make all your field goals all year then miss a game-winning one, and that's all people will remember."

But his performance dictated that the future was in his leg, not his arm. While he fell behind three starting pitchers in the Tigers' rotation, he was becoming the football Tigers' all-time leading scorer. He finished his college career with the most field goals kicked in school history.

IN THE HUDDLE

Gostkowski broke a 49-year-old team record with 158 points scored in 2013, the fifth most in NFL history, and led the NFL in scoring (156 points) and field goals made (35) in 2014.

Timing was also on his side in football. In 2005 the New England Patriots let kicking legend Adam Vinatieri go, which seemed like a really bad idea at the time, since he had won three Super Bowls with them, two of which came down to his last-second field goals.

But the Patriots have a way of unearthing diamonds in the rough and grooming replacements for team stalwarts. It's why they've won four Super Bowls under Bill Belichick.

In 2006, New England chose Gostkowski in the fourth round, 118th overall, and a perfect preseason by Gostkowski earned him a spot on the opening day roster.

Nine seasons later Gostkowski

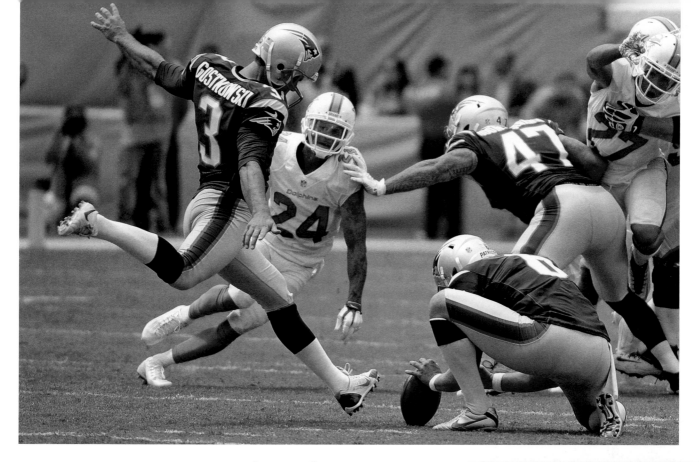

has eased past Vinatieri in the Patriots' record book. He holds the franchise marks for single-season field goal percentage and field goals made, career field goal percentage and consecutive games scoring. He also owns five of the seven highest single-season point totals in team history.

And while he was Second Team All-Pro to Vinatieri's First Team, in 2014 it was Gostkowski who led the league in points (156) and who made 35 of 37 field goal attempts, the most in the league. He also passed Vinatieri's New England record of 1,158 points to become the Patriots' all-time leading scorer.

"It's cool," said Gostkowski after breaking the record against the Miami Dolphins in December. "I have been put in a good situation, on a heck of a team with a great offense . . . Kicking field goals, you're only as good as the opportunities you're given. I try to take advantage of every one that

I'm given."

Gostkowski has played in three championship games with New England. The first two were agonizing losses, both to the New York Giants, and neither of them could be pinned on the kicker. In those two losses, Gostkowski was called upon only once to make a field goal — a second quarter, 29-yard chip shot for New England's first points in their rematch at Super Bowl XLVI.

In his third title game, Super Bowl XLIX against the Seattle Seahawks, Gostkowski excelled without much fanfare in one of the most exciting Super Bowls in history. He dutifully hit all his extra points and again didn't have a single field goal attempt. It's hard to generate the drama and historical highlight of a title-winning kick when you don't get the chance (as Vinatieri did).

But in a statistic that would excite only the deepest fantasy league nerds, kicking

fraternity or novelty bettor, all five of Gostkowski's kickoffs were touchbacks, making him the only kicker in Super Bowl history to prevent his opponent from returning a kickoff.

It is a fitting metric for a man who has quietly replaced and surpassed a kicking legend, and consistently leads his team in scoring — a team that also features superstars like Tom Brady and Rob Gronkowski.

CAREER HIGHLIGHTS

- First Team All-Pro (2008)
- Second Team All-Pro (2014)
- Three-time Pro Bowl selection (2008, 2013, 2014)
- Patriots' all-time leading scorer (1,179 points) and has the highest field goal percentage in team history and second-best in NFL history (86.8%).
- In 119 games, reached 1,000 points faster than any kicker in NFL history

ATLANTA FALCONS
★ ★ ★
RECEIVER\RETURNER
17

DEVIN HESTER

Devin Hester lived out a childhood dream in early February 2007 when he became the first and only player in NFL history to return the opening kickoff of a Super Bowl for a touchdown. A few years later, Hester surpassed even his wildest dreams when he set the all-time NFL return record.

As a young man, Hester's dreams were fueled less by hope and more by the need to escape the harsh reality that his father had died of cancer — when Hester was only 12.

Lenoris Hester had provided his son with many lessons and lasting memories, but the biggest legacy that remains with the talented kick returner is his father's speed. Legend has it that Lenoris once challenged the reigning Florida state 100-meter champion and had such a lead that he backpedaled the last five meters.

Using his father's gift, Hester starred at Suncoast Community High School in Riviera Beach, Florida, and by his senior year he was the top recruit in the state. With his pick of schools, Hester chose the University of Miami and became the first player in the modern history of the Hurricanes to play on offense, defense and special teams. He started games at cornerback, fullback, nickelback and running back, while also returning punts and kickoffs and getting spot duty as wide receiver.

"I've seen a lot of guys come through here," said Andreu Swasey, Miami's strength and conditioning coach. "But I don't think I've ever been around a guy this talented. You can't not find a position for him."

But that versatility worked against Hester because NFL teams didn't know where he fit in, thinking he was a jack-of-all-trades and master of none. Pundits said it was a wasted pick when Chicago chose Hester 57th overall in the second round of the 2006 draft.

IN THE HUDDLE

Hester holds the NFL records for punt return touchdowns (14) and combined punt and kick return touchdowns (20). He also had a 108-yard touchdown from a missed field goal that doesn't count towards the record.

They were quickly proven wrong. In Hester's rookie year he had six return touchdowns — no other player had ever reached more than four in a season — and he truly announced his arrival via *SportsCenter* in a November game against the New York Giants. Hester fielded a 52-yard missed field goal, took two steps as if he were going to concede a touchback, and then ran down the right sideline past the stunned Giants for an NFL-record-tying 108-yard touchdown.

That wasn't even the best part of the season. That moment came when he ran back the Indianapolis Colts' kickoff in Super Bowl XLI for a quick 7–0

lead. The Colts wisely kept the ball away from Hester for the rest of the game, and the Bears lost 29–17.

The following season, teams took the same tack and kicked away from Hester on 45 percent of their kicks, yet he still had six more return touchdowns (four on punts, two on kickoffs) and scored more points than any Bears receiver or running back.

With his strong hands, quick feet and knack for making people miss, Hester became one of the Bears' best options at wide receiver. But when his return touchdowns dwindled in 2008 and 2009, fans complained that he was being stretched too thin and should be focusing on returns. Hester disproved the theory: in the 2010 and 2011 seasons he played in every game, averaged 26.4 yards per reception and scored five touchdowns to add to the six he scored on returns.

In a 2011 win over the Carolina Panthers, Hester broke Eric Metcalf's career punt return record with his 11th touchdown. It had taken Hester 182 returns to reach the mark; Metcalf's 10 had come on 351 tries.

After years of electrifying runs, the Bears let Hester walk after he had just one touchdown from 2012 to 2013. The Atlanta Falcons grabbed the free agent in 2014, and his impact was immediate, catching five passes for 99 yards in his first game with the team — the second-highest total of his career.

Hester also scored the first rushing touchdown of his career in 2014 and was named to his fourth Pro Bowl. He also extended his own record with his 14th punt return touchdown and broke former

CAREER HIGHLIGHTS

- Four-time Pro Bowl selection (2006, 2007, 2010, 2014)
- Four-time All-Pro selection (2006, 2007, 2010, 2011)
- Three-time NFL Alumni Special Teams Player of the Year (2006, 2007, 2010)
- NFL 2000s All-Decade Team

Falcon Deion Sanders' all-time record with his 20th overall return touchdown.

"I'm overcome with emotions right now," said Hall of Famer Sanders in an interview with Hester after the game. "Because I love you as a man, as a father, as a husband . . . I'm so proud of you, man. I'm so proud of you. You know that."

ADAM JONES

Don't call him Pacman.

Adam Jones decided to shed that nickname — given to him for the way he went through milk as a child — in order to help himself truly become a man.

Born in Atlanta in 1983, Jones grew up with his mother, Deborah, and grandmother, Christine. When Jones was 4 years old his father was shot and killed in a robbery connected to drug dealing and criminal activities. His dad was only 24, and that was the longest a Jones man had made it in life.

This was the crucible from which Jones grew, and Christine believed that if her grandson made it past 25 he'd be okay.

Jones flunked out of two junior high schools, and on his first day at Westlake High School, Atlanta's football powerhouse, he got into a fight, which made him miss his first high school football game.

Once Jones got on the field, he was hard to stop. In his senior year he had 1,850 rushing yards, 120 tackles and six interceptions; he was named Conference Player of the Year and earned All-State honors.

At West Virginia University, Jones continued to excel on the field and to stumble off of it. His grandmother, the steadiest influence in his life, succumbed to cancer while Jones was a freshman. Alone and angry, he got probation for beating a fellow student with a pool cue. He also met his best friend, wide receiver Chris Henry.

As a junior in 2005, Jones was named a First Team All-American after leading the team in tackles (76). He was also named the Big East Special Teams Player of the Year for averaging 14.6 yards on punt returns and 23.4 yards on kickoffs. Jones declared for the 2005 NFL draft and was selected sixth overall by the Tennessee Titans. He started his NFL career by holding out for more money. His new teammates were not amused.

In 2006 they were a little fonder of Jones after he had an NFL-leading three punt return touchdowns to go with his four interceptions, one of which was a pick-six. Poised to be a star, he found new ways to sabotage his career.

IN THE HUDDLE

Jones majored in special education at West Virginia, and now works with the Special Olympics and coaches a special-ed basketball team.

At a gentlemen's club with his entourage and rapper Nelly in Las Vegas in 2007, Jones decided to rain $80,000 down on the dancers. A melee over the money broke out and shots were fired, paralyzing bouncer Tommy Urbanski.

In his defense, Jones said he didn't know the shooter — and he added that it was only $60,000. That didn't fly, and combined with other brushes with the law, Commissioner Roger Goodell suspended Pacman for the entire 2007 season.

Jones agreed to testify against the gunman for a lesser criminal

charge, and the Titans, happy to wash their hands of Jones, traded the oft-troubled kick returner to the Cowboys for a fourth-round draft pick. To prove he was a new man, Jones dropped the Pacman moniker and became the no-nonsense Adam Jones. But names really don't mean a thing, and Jones and the Cowboys were an ill-fated union. Dallas has a lot of strip clubs, and Jones was waived in 2009.

Without a team or much of a future, Jones also lost Henry, 26, to a car accident — another male in Jones' life who didn't make it through his mid-20s.

Coming off another year without football, Jones was given a chance to prove himself in 2010 with the Cincinnati Bengals. His season was cut short with a career-threatening neck injury, but he bounced back with a productive 2011 season. More important, he proved he had grown up a little, and the Bengals re-signed him to a three-year deal in 2013.

"Adam Jones . . . he's matured so much and changed and become a team guy," said Bengals defensive coordinator Mike Zimmer.

The year 2014 was one of redemption for Jones, as his undersized self-control started to catch up to his oversized talent. It was his fifth season in the Queen City, and he led the NFL in return average (31.3 yards) and was tied for third in punt return average (11.9 yards). That performance was good enough to get Jones his first All-Pro nomination, making the First Team as the best kick returner in the NFL. Now in his 30s, married to Tishana and the father of two daughters, Triniti and Zaniyah, he's reached an age and level of domesticity most never saw coming.

"This boy has gotten more patient, more understanding," says his mom. "He's grown up a lot. It's not all about him anymore . . . I think [the injury] changed him. It slowed him down a little bit."

But shades of Pacman still exist. In 2015 Jones was removed from a casino in Indiana for being disorderly. He apologized and chalked it up to a life lesson. Hopefully for Jones, he'll realize class is always in session.

PAT McAFEE

H̲e might wear No. 1 and be the top punter in the NFL, but Pat McAfee was No. 222 on draft day, and a few years prior, his odds of even making the draft were slim.

Still, McAfee had a hustler's confidence. In his senior year of high school in Plum, Pennsylvania — after being spurned by a promising-sounding scholarship offer — he borrowed $100 from a friend and bought in to an illegal poker game in the basement of a dodgy downtown restaurant.

Turns out he was as good a poker player as he was a kicker. He won $1,400, the amount he needed to fly to Miami and participate in a national kicking competition.

It was money well spent. McAfee nailed nine field goals in a row, moving further back each time until he finally missed at 70 yards — six yards beyond the NFL record.

McAfee's introduction to football was the local Punt, Pass & Kick competition, which his mother, Sally, had suggested he enter. Pat won, and as a sophomore in high school, he was the national champion.

McAfee had still never set foot on a football field in a real game, but Penn State offered him a spot in their summer kicking camp. By the end of the clinic, they told him he'd be given a scholarship.

Penn State reneged on that promise, and a devastated McAfee quit football. His father, Tim, took up his son's cause and sent highlights to all the Division I schools he could think of. Kent State was the only school that offered a scholarship, so McAfee accepted.

But Mike McCabe, the kicking guru who was hosting the competition in Miami, had also reached out to McAfee. With his parents encouraging him to simply stick with Kent State, Pat felt Miami could raise his profile. So he hatched his poker plan, flew to Miami and booted nine field goals.

After missing his 70-yard attempt, McAfee bolted the Miami camp to catch a flight. He didn't know that he won the competition. More important though, West Virginia University's recruiting coordinator followed him home and offered a full scholarship. It was the third free ride he'd been promised — and this one turned out to be the real deal.

In his four years as punter and kicker at West Virginia, McAfee had an average of more than 43 yards per punt and hit 58 field goals to set the school's all-time scoring record.

Despite that, McAfee wasn't invited to the NFL's scouting combine. So he set up his own and worked out for Dallas, New England and Indianapolis. The Indy special teams coach told McAfee he was only there because he'd been told to go.

"After that workout I said to myself, anywhere but Indianapolis," says McAfee.

The Cowboys said they'd select him in the 2009 draft. When they picked a USC kicker instead, it was

Penn State déjà vu. But a few hours later, the Colts drafted McAfee in the seventh round, 222nd overall.

The next day he and his dad went to work on his mechanics.

McAfee secured a spot on the Colts' roster in 2009, and was perhaps a little exuberant in celebrating his newfound fame. In 2010 he was charged with public intoxication, and the Colts suspended him for a game. McAfee issued a sincere apology to fans and teammates, and has since kept a clean profile — with the exception of tweeting a photo that happened to have a naked Andrew Luck in the background. The Colts fined him $10,000 and told him to wise up.

An avid Twitter user, McAfee has more than 300,000 followers. He also has the *Pat McAfee Show* on WTHR TV in Indianapolis, and appears regularly on the NFL Network and *The Bob and Tom Show.* With that kind of exposure, he's been called the "NFL's only celebrity punter."

After cutting junk food and 15 pounds, McAfee has also become the league's best. In 2014 he broke his own Colts records with 30 punts pinned inside the 20 and a net punting average of 42.8 yards. He was rewarded with his first selections to the All-Pro and Pro Bowl teams.

These results are one of the reasons his jersey is the Colts' second-best-selling one, behind Luck. McAfee also believes that Colts fans are savvy and respect the tactical importance of punts and field position. They also like that, at 6-foot-1 and 240 pounds, he can dish out some punishment, as Denver Bronco Trindon Holliday found out in 2013 after being demolished on a sideline return run.

McAfee thinks another reason his jersey is popular is because he was truly contrite after his arrest, and fans embraced that.

And he concedes there might be one more reason it's a top seller: "I still think people buy it because the No. 1 is slimming."

CAREER HIGHLIGHTS

- Holds Colts career records in punts (435), touchbacks (234), punting gross average (45.8) and punting net average (39.3)

- Broke his own franchise records for punts pinned inside the 20-yard line (30) and net average (42.8) in 2014

- Voted First Team All-Pro and to the Pro Bowl in 2014

DARREN SPROLES

Darren Sproles came into the world big. He was 10 pounds at birth and subsequently nicknamed Tank, a moniker that became ironic when he hit the NFL at 5-foot-6, 190 pounds. But as the old adage goes, you can't measure heart.

Sproles played big from an early age. His peewee football league passed a rule against running sweeps because Sproles scored a touchdown every single time he ran one; in high school he rushed for 5,230 yards (averaging 8.4 yards per carry) and scored 79 touchdowns.

In 2003, Sproles led the country in rushing during his junior season at Kansas State University, helping the Wildcats upset the heavily favored and top-ranked University of Oklahoma in the Big 12 Championship.

Sproles chose K-State to be close to his mother, Annette, who had been diagnosed with cancer. After finishing fifth in Heisman voting in 2003, he could have declared early for the NFL draft, but he chose to keep a promise to his mother that he would finish his degree.

Annette lost her battle with cancer at the beginning of Sproles' senior year, and though he played that season with a heavy heart, he finished his collegiate career with 23 school records. He also ranked 11th on the all-time NCAA rushing yards list and sixth in all-purpose yards.

Sproles earned his degree in speech pathology, a subject close to his heart because he'd always struggled with a stutter. It had affected his confidence and made him uncomfortable dealing with the media throng that had started following his gridiron success. It also endeared him to coaches and teammates, as much as his oversized achievements on the field did.

Sproles was drafted by the San Diego Chargers in the fourth round of the 2005 draft, and became a secondary and multipurpose offensive weapon behind LaDainian Tomlinson, then the best back in the game. In six years in San Diego, Sproles carried the ball 249 times for 1,154 yards (a 4.6-yard average), had 146 receptions for 1,400 yards, returned 25 kickoffs for 6,469 yards (a 25.1-yard average) and returned 114 punts for 935 yards.

In keeping with his nickname, Sproles also punched above his weight in blocking for Tomlinson and chewing up large chunks of the field. In a playoff game against the Indianapolis Colts in 2008, he accounted for 328 all-purpose yards (105 rushing, 45 receiving, 106 kick returning and 72 punt returning) and made the play on the winning touchdown in a 23–17 overtime victory.

In 2009 the Chargers placed the franchise tag on Sproles to hang on to him, but

in 2011 the New Orleans Saints signed him as a free agent. There, he replaced the departed Reggie Bush and reunited with former Chargers quarterback Drew Brees.

The chemistry between the two returned immediately. In his first game with the team, he returned a kick for a touchdown against the Green Bay Packers, and by his fourth game he already had more than 1,000 all-purpose yards.

Sproles also caught the pass that Brees threw to break Dan Marino's 27-year-old single-season passing record, and at the end of the season, Sproles had 2,696 all-purpose yards, an NFL record.

IN THE HUDDLE

Sproles leads the NFL with 15,045 all-purpose yards since 2007, and is second among active players in the category all-time (behind the Baltimore Ravens' Steve Smith Sr.).

"I had a lot of doubters in my first couple of years," Sproles says. "They always [said] that I'd be nothing more than a punt returner and a kick returner. So it felt good to get that record. It's always fun to prove people wrong."

The Philadelphia Eagles were believers and traded for Sproles in 2014 to replace the offense of DeSean Jackson, who had left to become a Washington Redskin. While Brees and the Saints were missing their little sparkplug, Sproles was enjoying life in the City of Brotherly Love with league-leading stats in punt return average (13.0 yards) and total punt return yards (506).

The numbers earned Sproles long overdue respect and recognition. He was named Second Team All-Pro and earned an invitation to the Pro Bowl as a punt returner. Both honors were a first for the dynamic back despite his leading the NFL in all-purpose yards (15,045) since 2007. Perhaps more stunning is that over the same time period, Sproles also leads all running backs in receiving yards (3,758) and receiving touchdowns (27).

"You have to understand something. As an athlete, Darren takes after me," says Sproles' father, Larry, who was a running back at MidAmerica Nazarene University. "But as a person, Darren takes after his mother. They both will fight for what they believe in. And nobody will ever stop them."

Just like a tank.

ADAM VINATIERI

Adam Vinatieri has some extraordinary genes. He was 42 during the 2014 season, his 20th in the NFL, and he was still the league's best kicker.

And there's ice in the family veins: Vinatieri's third cousin was legendary daredevil Evel Knievel, and his great-great-grandfather Felix, a 5-foot-2 Italian immigrant, was General Custer's bandleader.

After narrowly escaping the slaughter at Little Big Horn, Felix settled in South Dakota and started a family. Three generations later Adam found himself kicking footballs for Division II South Dakota State. Over his four college years he hit just 27 of 53 field goal attempts, but he still believed he could kick in the NFL. He was probably the only one who did.

Heeding the advice of Brian Hansen, a friend from South Dakota who was the New York Jets punter at the time, Vinatieri drove across the country to learn at the foot of Doug Blevins, a kicking guru who was born with cerebral palsy and coaches from a wheelchair.

Vinatieri lived in Abingdon, Virginia, for eight months, kicking on a high school field by day with Blevins and working at a restaurant by night.

Vinatieri still wasn't on the NFL's radar, so Blevins encouraged him to go to Europe and play for the Amsterdam Admirals in the summer of 1995. New England Patriots coach Bill Parcells took notice and invited Vinatieri to training camp in 1996. By the end of camp, he was the Patriots' guy. By the end of the season, he was in Super Bowl XXXI.

IN THE HUDDLE
Vinatieri holds the postseason records for most points scored (234), most field goals made (56), most field goal attempts (68), most extra points attempted and made (66 each), and most consecutive games scoring (29).

Vinatieri kicked only extra points in that championship game, a loss to the Packers, but the playoff experience was invaluable come the 2001 season. The Patriots, now with a young Tom Brady at quarterback, were playing the 2002 AFC divisional playoff against the Oakland Raiders in a New England snowstorm. As regulation time expired, Vinatieri kicked a 45-yarder in the swirling snow on a frozen field to tie the game 13–13. It's been called the greatest kick in NFL history, and he followed it up with another in overtime to send the Patriots to the AFC Championship Game.

Three weeks later the Patriots won Super Bowl XXXVI when Vinatieri hit a 48-yard field goal as time expired to beat the St. Louis Rams 20–17. Vinatieri also scored Super Bowl winning points for the 2003 championship (a 42-yarder to beat the Carolina Panthers 32–29) and again for the 2004 championship.

A lowball contract offer from the Patriots in the 2005 off-season forced Vinatieri to wade into free agency, where Indianapolis Colts coach Tony Dungy offered him a five-year, $12 million contract. Combined with the chance to kick in a dome and with Peyton Manning at quarterback, it was enough to seal the deal.

The following season the Colts were in Baltimore for a playoff game against the Ravens and their defensive wall. Manning couldn't find the end zone but it didn't matter: Vinatieri went 5 for 5 and scored all the Colts' points in a 15–6 win. The Colts went on to win Super Bowl XLI 29–17 over the Chicago Bears — Vinatieri's fourth in six years.

But the Colts and Vinatieri couldn't replicate the magic of that 2006 season again. Even when they did get back to the big game in 2009, Vinatieri was forced to watch from the sidelines — as he had for most of the season — after recovering from knee surgery. Worse, his replacement, Matt Stover, went only 1 for 2.

That was a lifetime ago, in NFL terms. Vinatieri is healthy, and the new-look Colts, led by quarterback Andrew Luck, are on the upswing. In 2014 they reached the AFC Championship Game, and although they lost badly to Vinatieri's former team from New England, the kicker did

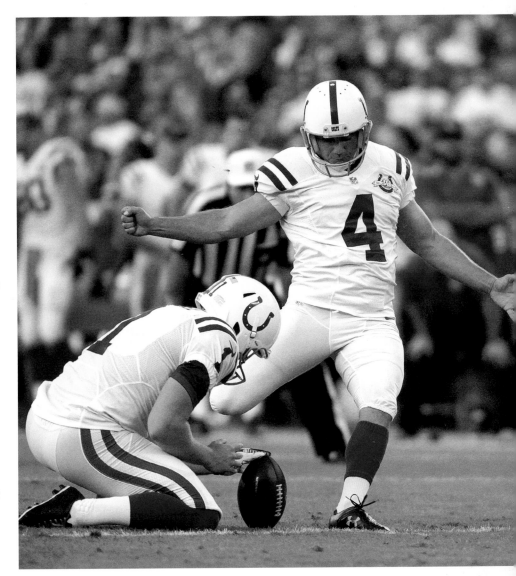

get a consolation prize: he broke Jerry Rice's record for postseason games played (Vinatieri had 30) and extended his record for consecutive postseason games scoring to 29.

As the ageless wonder soldiers on, he's burnishing his legend while helping the next generation follow in his footsteps. He serves as a mentor to Colts punter Pat McAfee, whom he encouraged to eat healthier and lose weight. Together they were the 2014 First Team All-Pro kicking unit — the best in the business.

"At some point, I'll be too old to do it," Vinatieri admits. "But that's a battle I'm not willing to give up just yet. The guys in this locker room, they really keep me young."

CAREER HIGHLIGHTS

- Four-time Super Bowl champion (XXXVI, XXXVIII, XXXIX, XLI)
- Three-time First Team All-Pro selection (2002, 2004, 2014)
- Three-time Pro Bowl selection (2002, 2004, 2014)
- New England Patriots 50th Anniversary Team
- NFL 2000s All-Decade Team

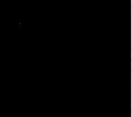

FRONT LINES

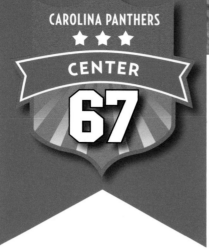

CAROLINA PANTHERS
★ ★ ★
CENTER
67

RYAN KALIL

Ryan Kalil's sense of humor, like his modest and quiet leadership, was a well-kept NFL secret — until Will Ferrell picked him to act in a skit.

After being named one of the league's 100 best players by the NFL Network in 2012, a segment was filmed in which fellow University of Southern California alum Ferrell, as alter ego Jackie Moon, teaches Kalil to protect a Twinkie from a defensive lineman.

Kalil grew up around football — not show business — in the Los Angeles area. His father, Frank, was a center who was drafted by the Buffalo Bills in 1982, and younger brother Matt is now a tackle for the Minnesota Vikings.

At Servite High in Anaheim, Kalil didn't allow a sack in his junior or senior seasons. As a USC Trojan he won the Morris Trophy, awarded to the league's top offensive lineman; he was a finalist for the Rimington Trophy, given to the nation's top center; and he was named USC's Most Inspirational Player.

Drafted in the second round, 59th overall, in 2007 by the Carolina Panthers, Kalil played right guard most of his rookie season. In 2008 he started 12 games at center and helped set a franchise record for fewest sacks allowed in a season, with 20.

In 2009, Kalil firmly established himself at center. He was one of

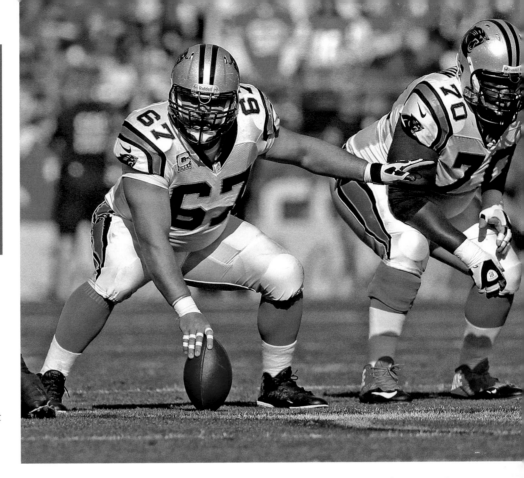

three offensive linemen to start every game and helped Jonathan Stewart and DeAngelo Williams become the first set of NFL teammates to both rush for more than 1,100 yards in a season. The team set franchise records with 525 rushing attempts and 2,498 yards, and Kalil was rewarded with his first trip to the Pro Bowl.

In 2011 the Panthers were seventh in the NFL and established team records with 6,237 net yards, 345 first downs, as well as 14 consecutive games with at least 100 yards rushing. The club tied for fifth in the league in scoring with 406 points, and ranked third in rushing with an average of 150.5 yards per game. Kalil was the man in the middle and earned his third straight Pro Bowl and first All-Pro selections.

After missing 11 games during the 2012 season with a foot injury, Kalil returned in 2013 to help the offense rank fourth in third-down efficiency, fifth in time of possession and second in drives lasting at least five minutes. He was named a First Team All-Pro selection for the first time, and hasn't missed a game since.

With the retirement of vocal leader Jordan Gross and three other offensive linemen prior to the 2014 season, Kalil became the elder statesman on a team that endured a rough year — including having eight different starting combinations on the offensive line. But with Kalil as the only constant, the Panthers

made it to the playoffs, beating the Arizona Cardinals before losing to the defending champion Seahawks.

"We did it because of Ryan Kalil," said offensive line coach John Matsko. "He's at that standard. Consistent performer day in and day out. You get a game-day performance out of this guy every single day. Every day is Sunday to him."

IN THE HUDDLE

Kalil's wife, Natalie, became (in)famous in her own right when, as a USC cheerleader, she was caught on camera inadvertently cheering for a University of Texas touchdown during the 2006 BCS national title game. The next Halloween she made light of the mistake by dressing up in a Longhorns uniform.

Rookie guard Andrew Norwell agrees. "He's been a leader in the offensive line room for I don't know how long. He gives me advice every day. That really means a lot to me

because he's looking out for me and wants me to be successful . . . Being a leader of the offensive line, being the center, making the calls and making sure we go the right way, that's a tough job. He's great at it."

It is this guiding nature that led to Kalil being named center on USA Football's All-Fundamentals Team in 2014, which recognizes players who "exhibit exemplary football techniques for youth players to emulate."

In 2014, Kalil landed on the NFL's Top-100 list again, and he didn't need to be Ferrell's straight man this time to stand out. He'd forgotten he was due to appear on the NFL Network to accept the honor, and when they reached him at home, he was in a bear costume playing with his daughter, Kenadi.

"I'm not happy," said Kalil to open the segment. "Two reasons. One, you took me away from my little girl. I literally got the call 20 minutes ago to come down and talk about this. We were playing Lions, Tigers and Bears. Obviously, I'm the bear. And two, I'm 93 on the list. That's BS. I want to see the voting."

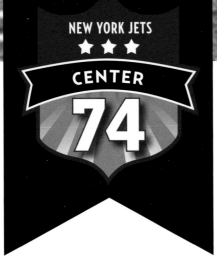

NICK MANGOLD

The center might be the hardest working man in football. He snaps the ball on every play and then immediately has to block a 300-pound opponent (or two) so that the recipient of the snap isn't crushed and his team driven backwards.

As these crucial plays are repeated, a synergy develops between the center and the quarterback, with the latter owing much of their success — and ability to walk off the field — to the former.

New York Jets center Nick Mangold, from Centerville, Ohio, is one of the very best in the NFL. He was a First Team All-State selection while playing both offense and defense for Archbishop Alter High School. At Ohio State University, he was a co-captain in his senior season and an Outland Trophy finalist after not allowing a sack the entire year. He also helped the Buckeyes generate 5,068 yards of offense — more than 422 yards per game.

It's a shame he hasn't had the same kind of team behind him in the NFL. Drafted 29th overall in 2006, Mangold was the first center in Jets history to start every game in his first year. Tackle D'Brickashaw Ferguson was drafted fourth that same year, and it was the first time since 1975 that a team took two offensive linemen in the first round. Together, Mangold and Ferguson are the only two offensive linemen in NFL history to start the first 75 games of their careers together.

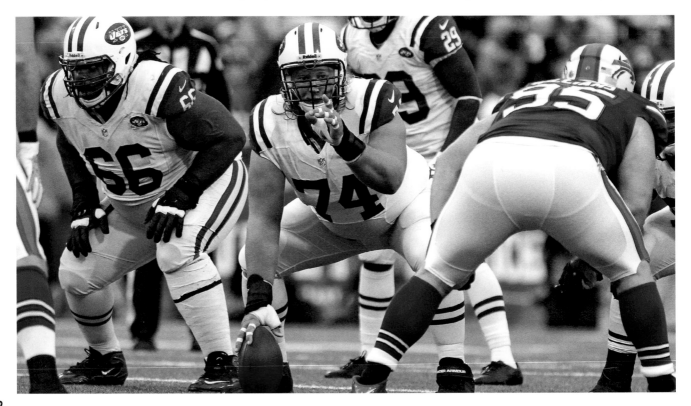

In 2009, as the Jets set a team record for rushing yards, Mangold made his first All-Pro team and second Pro Bowl. Heading into the 2010 season, Mangold was due for a raise. Negotiations dragged, but the Jets recognized the value of their star center and his chemistry with quarterback Mark Sanchez. While Mangold became the highest-paid center in the league, Sanchez proved to be less valuable and is now a Philadelphia Eagle.

IN THE HUDDLE
Mangold joined Jets owner Robert W. Johnson IV to commission the USS *New York*, which was built with steel from the World Trade Center.

While they were together, Mangold and Sanchez led the Jets to the AFC Championship Game in 2009 and 2010, but in 2011 Mangold missed the first two games of his career with a high ankle sprain. The Jets didn't make the playoffs and ended the season with an 8-8 record. Much of the blame fell on the shoulders of Sanchez.

True to form, Mangold defended his quarterback. "I know the guy had a rough go about it," he said after the season was over. "As an offensive line, in our group, we did not do the things to put him in a position to win. We did not protect him as well as we should have; we did not run the ball as well as we should have. Unfortunately, he kind of takes the brunt of the criticism,

even though we share in that blame . . . We should be taking most of it."

With the addition of quarterback Tim Tebow in 2012, Mangold started working in a quarterback platoon system, which he continues to do as the Jets now employ Geno Smith and Ryan Fitzpatrick at quarterback.

But if there's one man who can handle the multitasking, it's Mangold, who balances the different styles and talents of his quarterbacks while protecting them from the New York media hounds and the inevitable quarterback controversy that's part of the Jets' DNA.

In 2013 the Jets' record was 8-8, but they improved from 12th to sixth in the NFL in rushing. In 2014 the team fell to 4-12, costing coach Rex Ryan his job, yet they rose to third in rushing. That's not luck.

Mangold is the one constant in this equation. He has missed only one game over the last two seasons and has made the Pro Bowl both years, the fifth and sixth times he's been honored.

No blame for the Jets losing ways should be assigned to Mangold since he's one of their few stars and the epitome of consistency and reliability.

Plus he can't snap the ball *and* throw it.

"You're like the second quarterback," says Mangold of his position in the offense. "You get to see the chess game of a football game while it's happening. You get to be out into a leadership spot, and have guys look to you to make the right call. I like doing that."

TAMPA BAY BUCCANEERS
★ ★ ★

OFFENSIVE GUARD

70

LOGAN MANKINS

Offensive linemen are integral to a team's success, but the nature of the position often means they toil in anonymity. They're giants hiding in plain sight, but some, like Logan Mankins, manage to shine by virtue of their play and personalities.

Mankins grew up on a 10,000-acre farm in Catheys Valley, California, and dreamt of becoming a famous steer roper. His dream didn't come true, but his roping skills as an offensive guard, using leverage, strength and proper technique to protect his teammates from the animals on the other side of the line, have made him one of the NFL's best-known unknowns.

At Fresno State University, Mankins didn't allow his quarterback to be pressured or sacked during his entire senior season. At the All-Western Athletic Conference, he was the first offensive lineman to win the team's MVP award and was rated the top offensive guard prospect in the country by the NFL Draft Report — even though he played tackle in college.

The New England Patriots agreed and drafted Mankins with the final pick of the first round in 2005. He started at left guard in every game that year, the first Patriots rookie guard since 1973 to do so.

CAREER HIGHLIGHTS

- Five-time All-Pro selection (2007, 2010–2013)
- Six-time Pro Bowl selection (2007, 2009–2013)
- New England Patriots 2000s All-Decade Team
- New England Patriots 50th Anniversary Team
- Rated the best offensive guard prospect in college football by the NFL Draft Report during his senior college season
- First offensive lineman to be named MVP of the Fresno State Bulldogs

IN THE HUDDLE

Mankins won the 2012 Ed Block Courage Award, given annually to the player voted by their teammates as a role model of inspiration, sportsmanship and courage.

In 2007, Mankins made his first All-Pro and Pro Bowl teams after helping Tom Brady set the NFL single-season record of 50 touchdown passes. Those Patriots became the highest-scoring team in league history, and went undefeated during the regular season.

Mankins and the offensive line were even more important the following season, when Brady went down in the first game of 2008 with a knee injury and was lost for the year. The Patriots relied on their ground game — and for the offensive line to open the holes needed — and they finished the season ranked fifth in the NFL in

offense and posted 20-year franchise highs in rushing yards, rushing touchdowns and yards per carry.

The grunt work of the offensive line over Mankins' first four years (2005–09) partially enabled Randy Moss to set the NFL's single-season touchdown mark (23 in 2007) and Wes Welker to lead the NFL in receptions (112 in 2007 and 123 in 2009). Mankins was the leader of the group and its best player. By the time his rookie contract came to a close after the 2009 season, he had earned the right to be paid like a the star he'd become.

But negotiations were contentious. The Patriots designated Mankins their franchise player, blocking him from free agency while New England management continued to bargain. Mankins wasn't happy about their reluctance and held out for the first seven games of the 2010 season. And even though he played only nine games that year, he still made the All-Pro and Pro Bowl teams. On the eve of the 2011 season, he signed a six-year, $51 million contract that included a $20 million signing bonus.

Mankins' principles also led him to later file an antitrust suit against the NFL. Along with nine other players (including Brady), Mankins launched the suit as part of the complicated labor negotiations between the players union and team owners, which threatened to derail the 2011 season. Eventually, however, the players and owners came to an 11th-hour agreement that ensured football peace for the next decade.

But in a shocking move that proved who's boss in New England, Belichick and the Patriots traded Mankins to the Tampa Bay Buccaneers just prior to the 2014 season because he refused to take a pay cut.

"It's a business," Mankins said earlier in the year when asked about leaving dollars on the table to stay and play in New England, "and if you don't think it's a business, you're lying to yourself about that."

Brady was blindsided by the trade and upset with the move. Making matters worse, the Mankins-less Patriots allowed Brady to be sacked four times in Week 1 and were upset by the Miami Dolphins. Meanwhile, in his second game with the Buccaneers, Mankins cleared a path for little-known Bobby Rainey to rush for 144 yards.

Things worked out for the Patriots though, as they ended the season as Super Bowl champions.

New England's championship was a bitter pill for Mankins. Drafted three months after New England's third Super Bowl of the Brady-Belichick era, and traded five months before their fourth, the guard might be the most famous Patriot not to win a title.

Perhaps motivated by seeing his former mates win it all, Mankins showed up at preseason training in the best shape of his career. It bodes well for quarterback Jameis Winston, the first overall pick in the 2015 draft, who will lean on the veteran guard for guidance off the field as well as protection in the pocket while on it.

Mankins took care of the best of the last generation, and now he can lead the way for the next. Winston and the Buccaneers are fortunate to have his broad shoulders to rest their hopes and future on.

PITTSBURGH STEELERS
★ ★ ★
CENTER
53

MAURKICE POUNCEY

CAREER HIGHLIGHTS

- Two-time First Team All-Pro selection (2011, 2014)

- Two-time Second Team All-Pro selection (2010, 2012)

- Four-time Pro Bowl selection (2010–12, 2014)

- BCS National Champion (2009)

- Consensus All-America selection (2009)

The first thing LaShawn Maurkice Pouncey did after getting picked in the first round of the NFL draft was declare that his 82-year-old great-grandmother Ruth could quit her job cleaning houses.

Growing up in Lakeland, Florida, there wasn't always a lot of money in the Pouncey household, but there was plenty of love. Mother Lisa and stepfather Robert, who was a full-time fixture for Maurkice and his twin brother, Michael, from the age of one, always worked hard to keep food on the table and the boys on the straight and narrow.

Both Maurkice and Michael were a huge part of the offensive line at Lakeland High, where they won 45 straight games, three consecutive Class 5A State Championships and back-to-back USA TODAY national titles.

They stayed on the offensive line for the University of Florida Gators, where Maurkice started 11 of 13 games as a freshman in 2007 — a rare achievement. Originally a right guard, he played two games at center before making that his full-time position in his junior year.

Maurkice was a consensus All-American and the first player in school history to win the Rimington Trophy as the best center in college football. It was well deserved after not allowing a single sack or quarterback pressure that season, and he did it without being penalized once in the team's 919 offensive snaps.

Having also won the BCS National Championship with the Gators at the end of the 2008 season, there was little left for Maurkice to accomplish, so he separated from Mike and declared for the draft after his junior year.

While Maurkice was at Florida, stepdad Robert had lost his leg in a railroad accident and couldn't work. Leaving college a year early not only helped Maurkice's family financially, it also meant brother Mike could take over at center, his best position.

"I love Michael to death," Maurkice said after leaving school. "It's just amazing that you're always with somebody, but it's the time in our life now that we're separated and we're grown men and we got to go on about our lives."

Drafted 18th overall by the Pittsburgh Steelers in 2010, Maurkice quickly went about making a name for himself. He was the first Steelers lineman in a decade to start his first NFL game, and he won the Joe Greene Great Performance Award as the team's top rookie. By making both the Pro Bowl and Second Team All-Pro teams, Maurkice's talent was being recognized outside of Pittsburgh. He also received two votes for Offensive Rookie of the Year, almost unheard of for a center.

Pouncey's first five seasons have set him on the path to Canton — one blip aside. He missed the All-Pro and Pro Bowl teams in 2013 because of an ACL tear that he suffered eight plays into the season when his leg buckled under the weight of teammate David DeCastro.

"You think a guy like him is invincible," says left guard Ramon Foster. "For him to go down was a big shock more than anything. We had to rally and regroup with the new guys. It was something we had to get used to because he was always there."

IN THE HUDDLE
Pouncey was the first center in NFL history to be named to the Pro Bowl in each of his first three seasons.

The Steelers used three centers during the 2013 season, but Pouncey was back in 2014. Even before testing out his reconstructed knee, the Steelers signed him to a five-year contract extension that averages $8.8 million a season. His first year back proved it was money well spent, as he returned to his rightful place on the First Team All-Pro and Pro Bowl rosters.

"It's good to have our brother back," says left tackle Kelvin Beachum, who played some center in Pouncey's absence. "That's the biggest thing. He just brings a different attitude to the game. Everyone on this line has a different personality, and we feed off each other. It's great to have that centerpiece back in the middle. His personality was really missed."

And if Maurkice misses his brother, he has only to look to the AFC East, where Mike is now starting on the offensive line for the Miami Dolphins.

As for his brothers on the Steelers, "I'll do anything for this team," says Maurkice. "There's true love here."

TYRON SMITH

At 20 years of age, Tyron Smith was the youngest player in the NFL in 2011. He took over the right tackle position the day he joined the Cowboys, starting all 16 games of his rookie year. He was the first offensive lineman to start every game of his rookie season since Rob Petitti in 2005, and only the third in Cowboys history.

He allowed just three sacks that year, and Cowboys running backs averaged one more yard per carry when running behind him than behind the other linemen.

Smith moved to the left tackle position in 2012, a promotion on the offensive line to protect quarterback Tony Romo's blind side, and in 2013 his work there

earned him his first trip to the Pro Bowl and a Second Team All-Pro selection.

In 2014 the much-maligned Romo owed a huge debt of gratitude to Smith and his offensive line brethren. They were rightly praised for their protection, allowing him to operate in relative safety and reach the potential that

he'd been so frustratingly close to for years. Romo had career highs in touchdowns and quarterback rating, while running back DeMarco Murray led the NFL in rushing, breaking Jim Brown's record for 100-yard games to open a season and Emmitt Smith's single-season team rushing record in the process. Smith, Romo and Murray were All-Pro and Pro Bowl selections.

IN THE HUDDLE
Usually very quiet about his philanthropy, Smith and his girlfriend, Leigh Costa, have five rescue dogs, and together they created a 2015 calendar featuring Cowboys players to raise funds for a local dog shelter.

The result was a division-leading 12-4 record and Dallas' first playoff appearance since 2009, where they beat the Detroit Lions at home before losing to the Packers in Green Bay.

Smith rarely puts a wrong foot on the field, but he hasn't been immune to the challenges that exist for many players who come from little to reap the rewards of NFL stardom. In an all-too-familiar story, the money he had given his family when he signed his rookie contract was squandered, and his mother and stepfather wanted to buy a house that cost nearly three times as much as he'd told them he could afford.

"I love my family — I do — but I didn't love what they became," says Smith.

Torn between loyalty and self-preservation, Smith cut his family off in 2012. This ignited a feud, and family members have since been forcibly removed from his property and team facilities.

Smith's long-term contract came with a guarantee of only $22.1 million, and as the best young tackle in the game, it was viewed as a steal for the Cowboys. For Smith though, it was more about committing to a team that had become family.

Cowboys owner Jerry Jones, who has been there to help him through his family troubles, is especially important to him, and for a quiet, low-key guy who craves normalcy and security, he's very careful with what he does have.

"I know the amount of money I make in the NFL could be over any day," says Smith, who hasn't forgotten the hard work and value of a dollar from his days cleaning as a child. "It has to be put aside for me later down the line or for when I have a family."

Right now, he's taking care of his offensive family in Dallas, and the only thing they owe him is a debt of gratitude.

CAREER HIGHLIGHTS
- First Team All-Pro (2014)
- Second Team All-Pro (2013)
- Two-time Pro Bowl selection (2013–14)
- All-Rookie Team (2011)
- Morris Trophy winner (2010)

CLEVELAND BROWNS
★ ★ ★

OFFENSIVE TACKLE

73

JOE THOMAS

On draft day in 2007, Cleveland Browns fans were dreaming of a hotshot quarterback riding in from the University of Notre Dame to save their franchise. They were convinced the Browns would make Brady Quinn the third overall pick, and he would become an elite, championship-caliber quarterback, the way fellow Fighting Irish alumni Joe Montana and Joe Theismann had. Instead, they got Joe Thomas, a tackle from the University of Wisconsin, who was out fishing with his dad when his name was called.

A Joe-of-all-trades, in high school Thomas played right tackle, defensive end, tight end, fullback, placekicker and punter. He was heavily recruited as an offensive lineman by Notre Dame, the University of Michigan, Ohio State and the University of Nebraska. He decided to stay in his home state and play for Wisconsin, first as a blocking tight end and then as a left tackle.

Thomas was a starter from day one, and as a Badger he cleared the path for running backs Brian Calhoun and P.J. Hill Jr., who both had career years that season, gaining over 1,500 yards each before fading into obscurity.

During his junior year Thomas considered declaring for the NFL draft, where he was projected to be a top-15 pick, but at the end of the season, Wisconsin was playing in the Capital One Bowl and needed help on defense. Proving his versatility and commitment to the team, Thomas filled a hole at defensive end. Out of his normal position, he tore his ACL and his NFL dream took a serious hit.

Returning to Wisconsin for his senior year, it was clear Thomas' injury didn't have any lasting effects. He was named a consensus All-American and won the Outland Trophy as the nation's top lineman. Wisconsin won the Capital One

CAREER HIGHLIGHTS

- Named to the Pro Bowl eight times (2007–14)

- Five-time First Team All-Pro selection (2009–11, 2013–14)

- Two-time Second Team All-Pro selection (2008, 2012)

- Unanimous All-America selection (2006)

- Outland Trophy and Jim Parker Trophy winner (2006)

Bowl and ended the year with a 12-1 record — a school high for wins in a season — and ranked seventh in the country.

But Thomas' senior season was touched by tragedy. High school friend and ex-teammate Luke Homan went missing, and when Thomas heard the news, he left school and rushed to join the search party. By the time he arrived, Homan's body had been found in the Mississippi River.

IN THE HUDDLE
Thomas has now been in the Pro Bowl eight straight seasons, the only offensive lineman in history to be named eight consecutive years to start his career.

"Joe joined the search for his friend because Joe cares deeply about his family and those close to him," said Bret Bielema, Thomas' head coach in his senior season at Wisconsin. "He knew he wanted to do whatever he could to help find Luke, and he wanted to be there to comfort Luke's family and friends. Again, it speaks to Joe's character."

That character and personality fit Ohio's blue-collar work ethic perfectly, and Thomas' play quickly made him a fan favourite. He was second in Rookie of the Year voting and the only player not named Adrian Peterson to receive even a single vote.

Since 2006, Thomas' knee and the rest of his 6-foot-6, 312-pound body have held up against the grueling trench warfare of the NFL, and he has yet to miss a snap in his eight-year career, never mind a game. That's a mind-boggling 7,917 straight plays over 128 games — and counting.

Thomas met his wife, Annie, at Wisconsin and asked her on a canoe trip for their first date. According to her, there's a simple explanation for his consistency: "He loves football. He loves his teammates. All the

personal success, he's grateful for it. But he's the type of guy who doesn't let the bad or good get to him. I think that's why he's so steady."

The Browns wisely made Thomas the anchor of their offensive line, and the big left tackle showed his loyalty to the team by signing a six-year, $43 million contract before the start of the 2011 season.

The money didn't make Thomas soft. If anything, he's become more of a student of the game and a leader to the young Browns, teaching them football and life skills. As coach Mike Pettine said in reference to Thomas, "talent gets you to the league; character keeps you in it."

The fans in the Browns' Dawg Pound may have had their

reservations at the 2007 draft, but Thomas has proven that he's no average Joe.

While Quinn is now without a team, in 2014 Thomas became the first offensive lineman to make the Pro Bowl team eight straight years to start his career. His jersey went to the Hall of Fame to commemorate the occasion.

"I think any player that ever steps on a football field ends up dreaming about maybe someday having a piece of themselves in the Hall of Fame," says Thomas. "It's still kind of hard to believe. It's a pinch-me moment."

It's pretty certain that it won't be the last time the Hall calls and requests his presence.

MARSHAL YANDA

BALTIMORE RAVENS
★ ★ ★

GUARD/TACKLE

73

CAREER HIGHLIGHTS

- Four-time Pro Bowl selection (2011–2014)
- First Team All-Pro (2014)
- Two-time Second Team All-Pro selection (2011–2012)
- Winner of ProFootballFocus.com's 2014 Bruce Matthews Award, given to the best lineman in football

At his first Baltimore Ravens training camp, Marshal Yanda made a name for himself and won a few dollars at the same time by letting veteran Samari Rolle zap him with a stun gun.

"Easy money," said Yanda.

"I got shocked a bunch when I was working with electric fences on the farm. I used to run into them, get wrapped up, and they'd shock the crap out of you. I got used to them. It was the older fences that would really bite you, where you feel it on the end of your fingertips. There were a lot of volts there."

The family farm was in Anamosa, Iowa, northeast of Cedar Rapids, and it's where Yanda built his legendary strength and toughness by helping with backbreaking chores before the school day started. At Anamosa High he played on both sides of the line and was team captain and All-Conference, while also lettering in basketball and track and field.

After high school Yanda played for two years at North Iowa Area Community College in Mason City before spending two more years on the offensive line at the University of Iowa. In his senior year he was team captain, the offense's MVP, as well as the winner of the Hayden Fry Extra Heartbeat Award for leadership and dedication.

"Marshal is your typical Iowa lineman, a really tough kid with his technique down to a science," said former Chicago Bears director of college scouting Greg Gabriel. "He's considered an overachiever because he's undersized [6-foot-3, 305 pounds], but he's as good at what he does as anyone in the league."

Chosen in the third round — 86th overall — in the 2007 draft by the Ravens, Yanda was thrust into the lineup in the first game of the season when Jonathan Ogden got hurt. He ended up playing all 16 games.

The Ravens' success has long been based on a suffocating defense, but Yanda's protection on offense has helped the attack flourish.

As a rookie in 2007, Yanda and the offensive line helped the Ravens' quarterbacks set a franchise record with 341 passes for 3,308 yards. In 2008, Yanda suffered a knee injury and played in only five games. But in 2009 he helped the team set records for touchdowns (47) and rushing touchdowns (22) in a season, and the Ravens racked up 5,619 total yards, the third most in franchise history.

Yanda's grunt work lets the stars shine. In 2010 quarterback Joe Flacco completed 62.6 percent of his passes (306 of 489) for 3,622 passing yards, while setting career highs with 25 touchdowns and a 93.6 quarterback rating.

In 2011 it was Ray Rice who benefited from the holes in the line Yanda created. The running back led the league with 2,068 yards from scrimmage, set a team record with 15 total touchdowns (12 rushing and 3 receiving) and ran for a career-high 1,364 yards.

IN THE HUDDLE
Anamosa High School retired Yanda's number and named its weight room after him, and at the University of Iowa he won the Iron Hawk Award for feats of strength in the weight room.

Continuing the record-breaking trend, the Ravens set team marks in 2012 with 398 points and 5,640 total yards. In the postseason that year, Yanda fought through a serious rotator cuff injury to help Baltimore beat the San Francisco 49ers 34–31 in Super Bowl XLVII.

Five days after the game, Yanda underwent surgery. Even without the benefit of the weightlifting he's become famous for in the offseason, he still started every game in 2013. However, it was a down year for the offense and a letdown after their Super Bowl triumph, so before the 2014 season the Ravens hired offensive coordinator Gary Kubiak.

The new coach installed a zone-blocking scheme that revived the offense and took advantage of Yanda's versatility, which has seen him excel at both guard and tackle equally. The change spurred the Ravens' offense to greater heights,

as the group set franchise single-season records in yards (5,838) and points scored (409), and Flacco had career highs in passing yards (3,986) and touchdown passes (27).

The evidence of the improved offense continued in the 2014 postseason, but they ultimately lost their divisional playoff game against the eventual Super Bowl champion New England Patriots. However, Yanda helped Baltimore set even more marks. Playing out

of position at right tackle, he helped running back Justin Forsett rush for 129 yards (the third most in franchise postseason history), and Flacco tossed four touchdown passes to break the Ravens' record.

Yanda was named First Team All-Pro for the first time in his career in 2014, and made the Pro Bowl team for the fourth straight year, so being named winner of the 2014 Bruce Matthews Award was no great shock.

★ ★ ★

★ ★ ★

LINEBACKERS

SAN FRANCISCO 49ERS
★ ★ ★
LINEBACKER
53

NaVORRO BOWMAN

In 2010 the San Francisco 49ers had a middling defensive squad that ranked 16th in team defense out of 32 franchises. The next year, they vaulted to second-best defense in the league, which they repeated in 2012; in 2013 they finished third. A year later the defense was in tatters.

The rise of the 49ers defense coincided with that of NaVorro Bowman. Picked in the third round of the 2010 draft, he saw spot duty that year before he became the centerpiece of the dominant 2011 defense, leading the team in tackles and being named First Team All-Pro. It was the first of three straight years for both, as the 49ers knocked on the championship door but couldn't quite break through.

Raised in the crime-infested Washington, D.C. suburb of District Heights, Maryland, Bowman graduated from Penn State in three years with a degree in criminal law and justice. He also played for the Nittany Lions, registering in 93 tackles, including 17 for a loss, three sacks, two interceptions and two fumble recoveries in his junior and final year, earning him First Team All–Big Ten honors.

Bowman had been recruited out of Suitland High School in Forestville, Maryland, where he was

the state Defensive Player of the Year. His high school coach was Nick Lynch, a mentor and father figure who was killed in a car accident on the eve of Penn State's appearance in the 2009 Rose Bowl. Lynch's death came just six months after Bowman's dad, Hillard, died of complications from a blood clot.

IN THE HUDDLE

In December 2013, Bowman was named NFC Defensive Player of the Month after registering 56 tackles, three sacks, two forced fumbles, one fumble recovery and two interceptions. No other player achieved those numbers over the entire season.

"I use those guys," said Bowman in 2013. "I use those guys to get through every single day. When my father passed, I kind of wanted to throw in the towel. Just go home and do something to help my mom. But her being as strong as she is, she told me to stay in school, that my daddy wouldn't want me to quit. I carry that with me every day."

Bowman was dealt another heavy emotional blow after his father's death when he found out that Hillard wasn't his biological father. That man, Tracy Andrews, was killed when Bowman was a child. It was a secret Bowman kept for years following Hillard's death, but he revealed it in a 2013 episode of ESPN's *E:60*, during which he visited Andrews' grave and met family he never knew he had.

Bowman had a momentous year in 2013. In the final game ever played at Candlestick Park, he sealed a victory late in the fourth quarter against the Atlanta Falcons and set a team record for linebackers by returning an interception 89 yards for a touchdown. A week later against Arizona, he became the first 49er in 20 years to have a sack, a forced fumble, a fumble recovery and an interception in one game.

Many believed Bowman should've beaten out Luke Kuechly in 2013 for Defensive Player of the Year, and Pro Football Focus ranked him the best inside linebacker in the NFL, but he was hunting bigger game. Bowman wanted playoff redemption after the 49ers lost a 34–31 thriller to the Baltimore Ravens in Super Bowl XLVII the year prior.

But fate didn't have the same plans as Bowman. The 49ers lost the 2013 NFC Championship to the Seattle Seahawks, and Bowman's left leg gave way in gruesome fashion after Seattle receiver Jermaine Kearse landed on it, tearing his ACL.

Without Bowman in 2014,

the 49ers fell back to 10th in team defense, and they missed the playoffs. It cost coach Jim Harbaugh his job, and with the postseason retirement of mentors and All-Pros Patrick Willis and Justin Smith, the defense now belongs to Bowman. It's up to him to bring a little law and order to budding but troubled star Aldon Smith, who was suspended for nine games in 2014 for violating the NFL's personal conduct and substance abuse policies. Bowman, who was signed for $42.25 million through the 2018 season, understands he is in the right place to mentor Smith — both as a linebacker and a man.

"I'm not a saint. I've been around a lot of different things. But I know right from wrong, and I realized the opportunity I had before me," says Bowman.

"Not by any means do I take anything for granted. Every day I just thank God for everything and for how much success I'm having so early in my career."

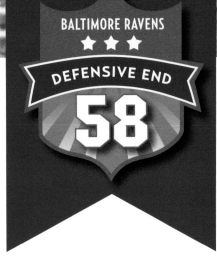

BALTIMORE RAVENS
★ ★ ★
DEFENSIVE END
58

ELVIS DUMERVIL

Six minutes cost Elvis Dumervil a million dollars a year, and he's okay with that.

"Doom" Dumervil had been a defensive end and linebacker for the Denver Broncos for seven mile-high years, and coming off 11.0 sacks and a career-high 54 tackles in 2012, Dumervil was owed $12 million in 2013.

The Broncos argued that Dumervil was overvalued and asked him to take a pay cut to help the team get under the salary cap. After talking with his agent, he agreed to re-sign for $8 million per season.

But the devil is in the details and nits were being picked. Dumervil got a revised offer at the 11th hour, which he had 35 minutes to sign and fax back before the 4 p.m. NFL waiver deadline. He and his agent say they sent the signed offer at 3:55 p.m.; the Broncos claim they didn't get it until 4:06 p.m.

Whoever was at fault, it was too late. The Broncos had sent their paperwork in at 3:59 p.m. to void Dumervil's contract and save their $12 million. He was officially a free agent.

The Broncos drafted Dumervil in the fourth round, 126th overall in 2006. Despite a stellar collegiate career at the

University of Louisville, where he led the country with 20 sacks in his senior season while also setting an NCAA record with 10 forced fumbles, his 5-foot-11 frame kept him from being a higher pick.

"It's always been like that," said Dumervil. "When I was in high school I had crazy numbers. I was supposed to go to Florida but something happened with that. Louisville wasn't where they are now. So I always had to go through the back door. My dad always told me history repeats itself."

IN THE HUDDLE
Since entering the league in 2006, Dumervil ranks fourth in the NFL in sacks with 90.0.

Dumervil was born in Liberty City, a rough-and-tumble Miami neighborhood. His father had been in the military and was a trainer and bodybuilder, and his mom worked for Marriott.

They separated when Elvis was three years old, and in middle school he moved in with his father and started playing football. His dad kept him off the streets by having him wake up at 5:30 in the morning to go for a run and work out; his mom took care of his spiritual upbringing.

Dumervil has 12 siblings, and six of the brothers played for Jackson Senior High School at the same time, including four on the defensive line. Two earned scholarships to Syracuse, and Elvis went with brother Curry to Louisville after being named All-State twice and having 30 sacks in each of his junior and senior high school seasons.

Curry was drafted by the Houston Texans and another brother, Louis, was picked by the New England Patriots. But Elvis was the best of them, and he showed it in 2009 when he led the NFL and set a Broncos franchise record of 17.0 sacks. He was named First Team All-Pro and played in the Pro

Bowl for the first time.

Riding high, Dumervil came crashing down in 2010, missing the entire year with a torn pectoral muscle he suffered before the season began.

The injury was eventually a factor in Dumervil's exit. After returning in 2011 he was put at defensive end in a new formation, instead of outside linebacker — the position he played in his record-setting 2009 season.

"I didn't complain. I did my job. I played hurt. I just wanted to win for those guys, the fans, the city. But then . . . they threw the fact I didn't have 15 sacks in my face."

After contentious negotiations and outdated communications technology cost the Broncos their sack machine, the Baltimore Ravens jumped at the chance to sign Dumervil as a free agent in 2013. His contract: five years and $35 million — $7 million per season.

To replace Dumervil, the Broncos signed pass-rushing monster DeMarcus Ware to a three-year, $30 million contract. Ware finished with 10 sacks in 2014, while Dumervil tied his career high with 17.0 sacks, good for third in the league and

CAREER HIGHLIGHTS

- Two-time First Team All-Pro selection (2009, 2014)
- Four-time Pro Bowl selection (2009, 2011–12, 2014)
- Broncos' Ed Block Courage Award winner (2011)
- Led the NFL in sacks in 2009 (17.0)

a new Ravens record. It was an impressive feat for a team long known to inflict their jersey colors of purple and black on opponents.

At the relatively advanced age of 31, Dumervil doesn't play every defensive snap these days, but Elvis has not left the building. He earned a fourth trip to the Pro Bowl and his second First Team All-Pro selection in 2014.

"I'm truly grateful, man. Great opportunity. Great organization. Great teammates. So many people played their parts," said Dumervil after breaking the Ravens' single-season sack record. "I'm just grateful to be in a great situation to be able to take advantage of it."

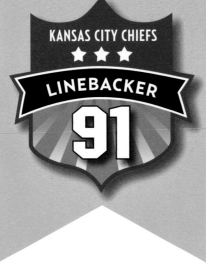

KANSAS CITY CHIEFS
★ ★ ★
LINEBACKER
91

TAMBA HALI

Born in Suacoco, Liberia, and raised in the capital city of Monrovia, Tamba Hali was six when war broke out in his homeland, forcing his family to periodically live in the wilderness to hide from the indiscriminate killing that was happening around them. In 1994, Hali escaped across the eastern border to the Ivory Coast with his sister and two half-brothers. They eventually made their way to Teaneck, New Jersey, to live with their father, Henry, who had left Liberia when Hali was two years old. His mother, Rachel, had never officially married Henry, so she wasn't eligible to be sponsored to come to the United States. It was 12 years before Hali saw her again.

English is the native language of Liberia, but Hali hadn't received a formal education and was functionally illiterate. He was also teased about his accent, but Hali discovered a home and a voice on the football field.

"I found myself enjoying myself when I was playing the game," says Hali. "Just being out there, having fun with my teammates . . . But I didn't even know about college scholarships. I was just playing to play. When I first got offered [a scholarship] by Boston College, I went to my

CAREER HIGHLIGHTS

- Two-time All-Pro selection (2011, 2013)
- Four-time Pro Bowl selection (2011–14)
- AFC sack leader (2010)
- 2006 NFL All-Rookie Team
- 2005 All-America selection at Penn State

coach and said, 'What am I supposed to say to the guy?'"

Hali ended up accepting a scholarship to Penn State University, aka Linebacker U, where he was a consensus All-American and the unanimous selection as the Big Ten Defensive Lineman of the Year in 2005. That season, he helped the Nittany Lions to an 11-1 record and a 26–23 victory over Florida State University in the Orange Bowl. If his achievements weren't enough to impress scouts, his speech at the 2006 draft combine was.

"I was just overwhelmed — not only with his story, but the way he told it," says Ernie Accorsi, general manager of the New York Giants the year Hali was drafted. "He's such a thoughtful, intellectual, moving person. You could hear a pin drop in our interview room when he was done telling his story."

The Chiefs drafted Hali 20th overall in 2006, which would have been the highlight of most football players' draft year — if not their lives — but Hali had other important things going on.

In July he left rookie camp for a day to be sworn in as an American citizen, and in September he saw his mother for the first time since he was 10 years old.

"I'm playing for her," Hali said before she was able to come to the United States. "Every time I get to the ball, every time I make my name more known, I feel like I'm closer to her."

IN THE HUDDLE

Hali is ranked second in Chiefs history with 31 forced fumbles, trailing only Hall of Fame linebacker Derrick Thomas (45), and Hali's 79.5 career sacks are the third most in team history.

As a rookie, Hali led the Chiefs with eight sacks — 3.5 more than the first overall pick, Mario Williams of the Houston Texans. After replacing all-world pass rusher Jared Allen on the right side in 2008 and then moving to outside linebacker in 2009, Hali had a breakout year in 2010, recording 14.5 sacks to lead the AFC. The Chiefs rewarded him with a five-year, $60 million contract, making him then the second-highest-paid outside linebacker in the league.

From 2011 through 2014, Hali missed only two games, playing 91 at outside linebacker and 50 at defensive end. He has 535 career tackles (414 solo), 79.5 sacks (minus-513.5 yards), 31 forced fumbles, seven fumble recoveries, 127 quarterback pressures, two interceptions and 15 passes defensed. He's made the Pro Bowl for four years running and has twice been an All-Pro.

After nine years there are a lot of miles on Hali, but he still managed to play all 16 games in 2014 with his usual zeal, recording 59 tackles and six sacks on a gimpy knee.

"He's got professional pride," says general manager John Dorsey. "I love everything that he's done this year . . . I like the person; I like how he plays the game of football."

For Hali, it's about earning your paycheck. "I believe in working," he says. "Me impressing myself is not really important. It's about working. Since I've been here, you really just don't say much, and you work, so success is going to come."

His story's been told, and his play has done the talking.

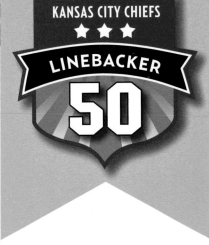

KANSAS CITY CHIEFS
★ ★ ★
LINEBACKER
50

JUSTIN HOUSTON

No name carries as much weight or is spoken with as much reverence among Kansas City Chiefs fans as that of Derrick Thomas. The best player in team history, he established all the franchise marks for sacks, as well as an NFL record with seven in one game.

Thomas died in 2000 at the age of 33 from a massive blood clot that formed after he was paralyzed in a car accident. He was named to the Hall of Fame posthumously in 2009.

It's a legacy that lives with the linebackers in Kansas City, and in Justin Houston the Chiefs have one who could threaten Thomas' records. He's already broken a big one.

After helping Statesboro High School win the Class 4A Georgia state title in 2005, Houston went to the University of Georgia, where he had a total

CAREER HIGHLIGHTS

- Three-time Pro Bowl selection (2012–14)
- First Team All-Pro (2014)
- NFL sack leader (2014)
- AFC Defensive Player of the Month (September 2013)

of 125 tackles (70 solo), 20.0 sacks (negative 134.0 yards) and 38.0 tackles for loss (negative 168.0 yards).

Projected to be a first-round pick after skipping his senior year to enter the draft, Houston fell to the third round in the 2011 because he tested positive for marijuana before the NFL scouting combine.

IN THE HUDDLE
Houston is one of only 10 players with 20.0 sacks in a season, and he's had more sacks in his first four seasons (48.5) than all but seven players in NFL history.

In an interview before the draft, Houston discussed the situation with the Chiefs, who took him 70th overall.

"I feel like I was very honest with them. Just told them it was a mistake that I had made. I'm putting it behind me. I'll do whatever they want me to do. I think they trust me. They took a chance, and I'm going to make them proud for taking a chance."

Some scouts also wondered about his true position (defensive end or linebacker) and if he put in maximum effort on every down. But you won't survive in the NFL if you don't, and Houston dispelled the laziness myth in his rookie year. He played all 16 games in 2011, had 56 tackles, 5.5 sacks and six special teams tackles, and won the Mack Lee Hill Award, given to Kansas City's best rookie or first-year player.

In 2012, Houston upped his numbers to 66 tackles and 10.0 sacks, and he started strong in 2013, winning AFC Defensive Player of the Month in September — the first Chief to win since Thomas in 1997. That month included a career-high single-game 4.5 sacks in

a win over the Philadelphia Eagles. But his season was derailed by an elbow injury that caused him to miss the final five contests of the year.

Back at full strength in 2014, Houston recorded 68 tackles (58 solo and 23 for loss), 25 quarterback pressures and four forced fumbles. And he saved his best for last, getting four sacks in a 19–7 win over the San Diego Chargers in the 2014 season finale, sewing up the NFL sack title for the year with 22.0. The total surpassed Thomas' 20.0 sacks to set a new franchise record, but fell half a sack short of Michael Strahan's 13-year-old NFL single-season mark.

Breaking that record was within reach, but Houston put his team ahead of individual accomplishment: "The last couple of plays that coach

called were for me to drop. It's a team game."

It might be sacrilegious in Kansas City to say so, but Houston is challenging Thomas as the best pass rusher in Chiefs history. He is arguably a more complete player — stronger against the run than Thomas was — and he has the ability to drop into coverage and defend receivers too. As respected stats-analysis website Pro Football Focus tweeted in 2014, "Justin Houston has +104.2 overall grade since coming into NFL in 2011, best of any 3-4 OLB [outside linebacker] during that span." This means simply that in Pro Football Focus' grading analytics, in which the average is a zero score, Houston has time and again overachieved.

Even without advanced stats, the Chiefs know Houston is a once-in-a-generation player.

CAROLINA PANTHERS
★ ★ ★
LINEBACKER
59

LUKE KUECHLY

Luke Kuechly, pronounced "KEEK-lee," is a tackle machine and record smasher, and very few saw it coming. Not even his parents were convinced of his talent.

Growing up in Evendale, Ohio, a comfortable suburb north of Cincinnati, Kuechly played for St. Xavier High School, a team that went undefeated and won the state championship in his junior year. After the triumph, Kuechly's coach Steve Specht told parents Eileen and Tom to expect a lot of interest from college football coaches. Eileen says she remembers thinking, "You don't know what you're talking about. That's crazy."

But Specht did know. The University of Cincinnati offered Kuechly a scholarship after his dominant senior year playing a cross between a linebacker and a safety off the line of scrimmage. But he didn't want to stay so close to home, and when calls didn't come from logical choices Notre Dame or Ohio State — possibly because he wasn't fleet enough for safety or big enough for linebacker — an uncle suggested he seek the best education possible.

After considering Duke and Stanford, Kuechly chose Boston College. He left school with 532 tackles — the second most in NCAA history — and he's the only player to ever lead the nation in tackles twice, averaging an NCAA-record 14.0 a game. He also set a record with at least ten tackles in 33 straight games.

As a junior Kuechly won the Bronko Nagurski Award as the nation's top defensive player, the Butkus Award as most outstanding linebacker, the Rotary Lombardi Award as the best lineman or linebacker, and was named First Team All-American. Forgoing his senior season, Kuechly was drafted ninth overall by the Carolina Panthers in 2012.

IN THE HUDDLE

Kuechly is the second player in NFL history to win the Defensive Rookie of the Year and Defensive Player of the Year in back-to-back seasons (after Lawrence Taylor in 1981 and 1982), and just the eighth to win both.

Kuechly played the first four games of his rookie year as the weakside linebacker, moving into the middle when Jon Beason was injured. Before the switch, the Panthers were ranked 24th in the league defensively; afterwards, they were 10th. He played every snap of the last 12 games as middle linebacker and led the league in tackles with 164, which also broke the NFL rookie record.

The single-game NFL tackle record is debated, but it's believed Kuechly tied the mark with 24 tackles in the 2013 season finale against the New Orleans Saints. The Panthers had him down for 26 after reviewing the game tape, but it's not official. Kuechly also had an interception that day for good measure.

Kuechly didn't lead the NFL in tackles in 2013 — he was fourth — but Carolina was second in the league in total defense and points allowed. For his part, Kuechly was named Defensive Player of the Year, one year after being named the Defensive Rookie of the Year.

Back at the top of the NFL tackle board in 2014 for the second time in three seasons, Kuechly has more tackles (473) than any other player since he joined the league, and the Panthers' defense has been ranked in the top 10 in each of his three seasons. He's also been on the All-Pro First Team and in the Pro Bowl each of the last two years.

That kind of success usually draws the bright media spotlight, riches and an entourage, but Kuechly keeps a pretty low profile. It helps — or hinders, depending on your perspective — that he plays in a small market in Carolina. His humility is a reflection of his upbringing. At home there are no shrines to his football achievements, only pictures of him and his two brothers, John and Henry.

Off the field Kuechly hangs out with older, married teammates and was content to use the Wi-Fi in his building's common area until recently. He has a Twitter account but has posted only a handful of tweets since he opened it in 2013. And Pepsi, one of his few endorsements, had fun with his straightlaced persona, trying

CAREER HIGHLIGHTS

- Defensive Player of the Year (2013)
- Defensive Rookie of the Year (2012)
- Two-time First Team All-Pro selection (2013–14)
- Two-time Pro Bowl selection (2013–14)
- Two-time NFL tackle leader (2012, 2014)

unsuccessfully to create a nickname for him in his first TV spot.

On the field is a different story.

"The guy is a stud," says Saints quarterback Drew Brees, who knows a thing or two about facing elite defenders. "He is all over the place. He seems like he's making every tackle and every call. He's as good a football player as there is in the league."

Even his mom came around, saying to Specht after her son was drafted, "I have to apologize to you because I thought you were nuts."

DeANDRE LEVY

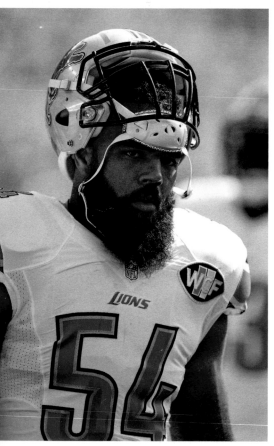

DeAndre Levy is not your average linebacker. He sports a beard that falls somewhere between logger and hipster, and he spends the first half of his off-season traveling far off the beaten path to places like the Amazon, where his sustenance includes frogs and rats.

He also doesn't play like a typical linebacker, which has made Levy the poster boy for the modern hybrid defensive player. His unconventional game, however, has cost him some adulation outside Detroit's locker room.

The second half of Levy's off-season is typically spent at home in Wisconsin, where he trains for the upcoming season. He's one of the smallest linebackers in the league but one of the strongest, and one of the best. He regularly outperforms fellow NFL players in the gym.

At Vincent High School in Milwaukee, Levy was a three-time team captain, two-time team MVP and a First Team All-State as a senior. He also showed up on the offense in his final year, catching 12 passes for 260 yards and three touchdowns.

Levy chose to stay in state and go to the University of Wisconsin, where he was a strong-side linebacker who blitzed, but also had the speed to drop back and cover receivers. As a Badger he had 211 tackles (116 solo), 15 sacks for minus-105 yards, 28 stops for loss (totaling 155 yards) and 10 quarterback pressures. He also caused six fumbles and recovered six more, returning one 45 yards; he deflected seven passes, intercepted two and blocked a kick. In short, on defense Levy did it all.

In 2008, Levy was given the Tom Wiesner Award, for the senior football player who most exemplifies leadership and courage, and in 2009 the Detroit Lions drafted him in the third round, 76th overall. His stock had fallen after a subpar performance at the NFL scouting combine, a result of some back trouble and training injuries. But that didn't affect Levy's performance when he arrived in Detroit, playing all 16 games his rookie year. He became a starter midway through the season, and at the end of the year was given the Chuck Hughes Most Improved Player Award by his teammates.

IN THE HUDDLE

Levy was ranked 59th-best player in the league in 2014 by his peers, and ProFootballFocus.com graded him as the NFL's best linebacker against the run with the highest run stop percentage: he makes a defensive stop on 16.6 percent of run plays he's on the field for.

Re-signed by the Lions as an unrestricted free agent in 2013, Levy repaid the team's faith: he was second on the team in tackles with a career-high 118 (85 solo), had a career-high 16 passes defensed and six interceptions. His interception total made him the third Detroit linebacker to record six picks in a season and the first since Hall of Famer Joe Schmidt in 1958.

When throwing Levy's way in 2013, quarterbacks had a miniscule 57.5 passer rating and just one touchdown against those six interceptions. It was a performance that made him the second-most effective pass defender in the league, behind superstar Richard Sherman of the Seattle Seahawks.

Surprisingly overlooked in year-end NFL honors, Levy was voted by his teammates winner of the 2013 Lem Barney Award as the Lions' defensive MVP.

The 2014 season was even better. Levy started by recording 10 tackles (nine solo) and an interception in Week 1, which earned him the NFC Defensive Player of the Week award, and he went on to take the NFC Defensive Player of the Month for September. He finished the season with a career-best 151 tackles (117 solo), 2.5 sacks, five passes defensed and his first career safety.

Often overshadowed by Ndamukong Suh, his defensive linemate from 2010 to 2014,

NFL.com writer Chris Wesseling ranked Levy fifth, one spot ahead of Suh, in his top-10 candidates for 2014 Defensive Player of the Year.

According to Wesseling: "Levy has been perhaps the most complete linebacker in the league, going sideline to sideline tracking down the run, covering tight ends and scatbacks and making plays behind the line of scrimmage."

When it came to All-Pro selections, Levy's versatility worked against him, and voters couldn't decide whether he was an inside or outside linebacker, having started at both. He split his own vote and appeared in more than one category, making it on the Second Team as an inside linebacker.

And he might start showing up on the ballot for more positions. Using a linebacker to cover a wide receiver in the red zone is something most defensive coordinators wouldn't risk losing their jobs for, but the Lions weren't afraid to put the 6-foot-2, 235 pound Levy up against All-Pro

CAREER HIGHLIGHTS

• Second Team All-Pro (2014)

• NFC Defensive Player of the Month (September 2014)

• Winner of the Lem Barney Award as the Detroit Lions' defensive MVP (2013)

Jordy Nelson on a game-clinching play against the division rival Green Bay Packers in 2014.

"The trend to go more wide open on offense [forces you] to have some linebackers who can play in space," says Lions defensive coordinator Teryl Austin. "DeAndre is an every down linebacker for us, whereas a lot of teams will put six defensive backs on the field and have one playing linebacker. Fortunately, we don't have to do that."

As Lions safety Glover Quin puts it, "DeAndre covers better than a lot of safeties."

GREEN BAY PACKERS
★ ★ ★
LINEBACKER
52

CLAY MATTHEWS

CAREER HIGHLIGHTS

- Five-time Pro Bowl selection (2009–12, 2014)
- First Team All-Pro (2010)
- Second Team All-Pro (2012)
- NFC Defensive Player of the Year (2010)
- Dick Butkus Award (2010)

Clay Matthews III is the scion of football royalty, but that doesn't mean the game came easily or that his path to the NFL was assured.

Clay Sr. played defensive end for four seasons with the San Francisco 49ers in the 1950s, and Clay Jr. was a linebacker with the Cleveland Browns and the Atlanta Falcons from the late-1970s through the mid-1990s. (Uncle Bruce was the best of them all, playing 19 seasons with the Houston Oilers franchise.) Growing up, however, there was little indication that Clay III was going to make his family only the second in history to have three generations of NFL players.

As a junior at Agoura High School in Agoura, California, Matthews weighed 166 pounds soaking wet, which is the main reason his father, the team's defensive coordinator, kept him off the field. After a growth spurt, in his senior season he became a starter for the first time, but there was no college recruitment to speak of.

Matthews enrolled at the University of Southern California anyway, trying out for the Trojans as a walk-on. After sitting out a year, he earned a scholarship in his sophomore season, but it was a loaded USC team, and as in high school he didn't become a starter until his senior year.

Even as a late bloomer, Matthews played in four straight Rose Bowls, was named a USC Special Teams Player of the Year three times and in the Senior Bowl had a game-high six tackles, including a sack, two fumble recoveries and a forced fumble. It was an impressive showing that prompted the Green Bay Packers general manager Ted Thompson to break with his own tradition and trade up into the first round to get Matthews, who was picked 26th overall in 2009.

IN THE HUDDLE
Matthews is the first player in Packers history to earn Pro Bowl recognition in each of his first four seasons in the league (2009–12), and the first to score a defensive touchdown in each of his first three seasons.

A hamstring injury held Matthews back in training camp and the preseason, but he burst onto the NFL scene with a first year to remember. Playing all 16 games, Matthews set a franchise rookie record with 10 sacks and became the first freshman to lead the team in quarterback takedowns since 1986. He was also the first Green Bay rookie since 1978 to be named to the Pro Bowl.

Avoiding the sophomore slump, Matthews upped his numbers in his second season, with 13.5 sacks and 40 quarterback hits. He also had his first career interception, which he ran back for his first touchdown during a prime-time game against the Dallas Cowboys.

That was merely a prelude to the postseason and an unlikely Super Bowl run. The Packers won their final regular season game to squeak into the playoffs, and then won three road games to reach the Super Bowl, in which Matthews had 3.5 sacks, a franchise record for one postseason. In Super Bowl XLV against the Pittsburgh Steelers, he topped it with the most important defensive play of the season.

At the start of the fourth quarter, the Packers were clinging to a 21–17 lead with the Steelers driving. Anticipating a run, Matthews told defensive end Ryan Pickett to push the runner outside, where Matthews met Pittsburgh's Rashard Mendenhall with a high hit that knocked the ball loose. Green Bay recovered the fumble and scored a touchdown on the ensuing drive, which ultimately made the difference in their 31–25 victory. And Matthews did it all on a broken leg.

"I don't make a big deal of it," he said. "[It happened] sometime in the middle of the season. You can't do anything about it. I was just taking practices off and showing up on game day and giving it my all."

You don't play with the kind of violent abandon that Matthews does and not suffer, and in 2013 he missed five games with a broken thumb. He still tied team and career highs with three forced fumbles, and led the Packers with 7.5 sacks.

In 2014, Matthews played all 16 games for the first time since his rookie year and had a career-high 61 tackles to go with 11.0 sacks and his fifth Pro Bowl selection. And with a sack against the Seattle Seahawks in an overtime loss in the NFC Championship, he also surpassed Packers legend Reggie White for the most postseason sacks in franchise history.

Younger brother Casey is on the Minnesota Vikings, and cousins Kevin and Jake play for the Carolina Panthers and Atlanta Falcons, respectively. But Clay is the best of the Matthews bunch, and if he continues his stellar play, he is certainly making a case to join his uncle Bruce in the Hall of Fame.

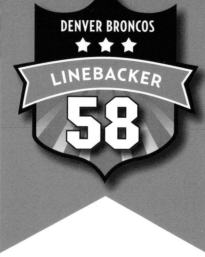

DENVER BRONCOS
★ ★ ★

LINEBACKER

58

VON MILLER

Vonnie B'Vsean Miller was built to play football. At 6-foot-3 and 250 pounds, he's a rare blend of speed and power, with the ability to outmaneuver or drive past the monsters on the offensive line.

Better known as Von, Miller grew up in DeSoto, Texas, where he was one of the best defensive end prospects in the state. He accepted a scholarship to Texas A&M University, and following his freshman year, former Green Bay Packers coach Mike Sherman took over the program. Suddenly he could no longer get by on raw talent alone.

One of Sherman's first acts was to suspend Miller until he started taking practices and schoolwork seriously. Miller considered transferring, but his father reminded him he had made a commitment to the university and the team. With renewed purpose, he put his nose to the grindstone.

Miller paid almost immediate dividends after being welcomed back from his suspension. In his junior year he was installed as a hybrid defensive end/outside linebacker, a position that was called *joker*. That season, Miller led the country in sacks with 17 and was fifth with 21.5 tackles for loss.

In his senior year Miller battled an ankle injury, but his 10.5 sacks and 17.5 tackles behind the line of scrimmage still earned him the Butkus Award as the country's best linebacker.

After being drafted second overall in 2011 by the Denver Broncos, Miller

added to his trophy shelf in his rookie year: he was named to the All-Pro and Pro Bowl teams and won Defensive Rookie of the Year.

"I'm going to attack and give relentless effort, fanatical effort," said Miller. "That's my formula, and I'm sticking to it. I try to get off the ball as fast as possible and react to whatever the offense is trying to do to me. I don't really have any premeditated moves."

IN THE HUDDLE

Miller holds the Broncos franchise record for sacks in a season (18.5 in 2012), and his 49.0 sacks after four seasons are more than all but four players in NFL history — Reggie White, Derrick Thomas, J.J. Watt and Dwight Freeney.

In 2012, Miller was runner-up for Defensive Player of the Year after setting a Broncos single-season record with 18.5 sacks. He finished the year ranked in the top 5 in quarterback knockdowns (27), quarterback hurries (12), tackles for loss (28), run stuffs (13) and forced fumbles (6). He also became one of only two players since at least 1994 with 15 sacks, 25 tackles for loss and five forced fumbles in a single season. The other player was current teammate DeMarcus Ware, who did it with the Dallas Cowboys in 2008.

While ranked the ninth-best player in the NFL Network's annual Top-100 list prior to the 2013 season, Miller was suspended before the season opener for spilling his urine sample and submitting a diluted one — a common tactic to fool a drug test. It was his second violation of the NFL substance abuse policy (the first was for marijuana and amphetamine use), and it meant a six-game suspension.

"Although my suspension doesn't result from a positive test, there is no excuse for my violations of the rules," Miller said in a statement.

He later added, "I've just got to grow up, be more mature and take care of business."

With Peyton Manning leading a record-breaking offense, the Broncos won their first six games without Miller and rolled to Super Bowl XLVIII. Miller was forced to watch from the sidelines after he tore his ACL in the second-last game of the regular season, and Russell Wilson and the Seattle Seahawks ran roughshod over the Denver defense in the 43–8 Super Bowl victory.

With an off-season of rehab and reflection, Miller returned focused in 2014. "I think that he has grown up a lot," says John Elway, Broncos general manager and executive vice president of football operations. "He's done a tremendous job of doing the right things and everything he's supposed to be doing."

Von played all 16 games in 2014 and had 14.0 sacks and 59 tackles, earning his third trip to the Pro Bowl and his third All-Pro selection. Pro Football Focus' advanced metrics ranked him as second-best linebacker in the NFL in run defense and pass rushing, and the 24.0 sacks he had along with Ware were more than the total of the Falcons, Raiders and Bengals combined.

Miller played clean and lean; he was a sleeker version of himself after losing weight to be more explosive and have less stress on his joints.

"A Ferrari isn't built to carry luggage to and from the airport," explained Miller.

★ ★ ★

DEFENSIVE END

92

HALOTI NGATA

Haloti Ngata (pronounced "ha-LOW-tee NAH-tah") was named after his uncle, which is a family custom in Tonga, where Ngata's parents, Solomone and Olga, grew up.

The pair immigrated to the U.S. in search of greater opportunity for their future family. Haloti was born in Inglewood, California, and went to Highland High School in Salt Lake City, where he was named Utah Player of the Year in 2001.

After considering Brigham Young University, Ngata, a devout Mormon, decided to go to the University of Oregon, where as a junior he was a consensus All-American and finalist for both the Outland Trophy and the Bronko Nagurski Trophy.

Sadly, Ngata's parents — his role models and biggest fans — didn't live to see his NFL success. During his freshman year at Oregon, his father, who had seen every one of his games — both home and away — died when his work truck slid off an icy road, and he drowned. And just after his junior season, his mother passed away from diabetes complications — and some say a broken heart.

His mother's health played a major factor in Ngata's decision to enter the NFL draft a year early. He had considered leaving school to be by her side but thought an NFL salary would be the best way to take care of her, so he asked for her blessing. She agreed 12 days before passing away.

Three days after her funeral, Ngata went to Houston with uncle Haloti Moala to prepare for the draft.

"This had always been his dream, and he wanted to follow through on it, especially because his mother had supported it," said Moala. "Football kept him going when his father died, and it's done the same for him through his mother's death."

Ngata continues to honor his parents through the hard work and diligence they taught him, and by carrying on Tongan traditions like the Haka — a dance that awakens the warrior within and hones his balance, footwork and dexterity.

IN THE HUDDLE

Ngata was part of a Ravens defense that did not allow a 100-yard rusher in 39 straight games, and since he entered the NFL in 2006, the Ravens have allowed the fewest rushing touchdowns in the NFL (71).

"For me, the Haka is calling upon my ancestors to have their spirits with me on the field," says Ngata. "It makes me feel closer to my culture."

The Baltimore Ravens traded up to select Ngata 12th overall in 2006, and even at 6-foot-4 and 340 pounds, he's one of the NFL's most athletic defensive tackles. He stops the run (528 career tackles), rushes the passer (25.5 career sacks for a loss of 192 yards) and even covers receivers — his five career interceptions are the most by a

defensive tackle since he entered the league.

In 2011, Ngata led the NFL's third-ranked defense (which was second against the run and best in the league in the red zone) with 64 tackles, 5 sacks for a loss of 21 yards, 3 fumble recoveries — including his first for a touchdown — and 2 forced fumbles. But despite his brilliance, the 2011 club went home losers after the AFC Championship Game. It was the second time in his career that Ngata was one game away from the big dance.

In 2012 he finally made it. Super Bowl XLVII featured the Ravens against the San Francisco 49ers and quicksilver quarterback Colin Kaepernick. With the Ravens up 28–13, Ngata went down with a sprained MCL on a Frank Gore scoring drive. Operating a little more freely, San Francisco mounted a comeback, but the Ravens held on to win, and Ngata was finally a champion.

From 2011 to 2014, Ngata was the only defensive tackle in the league who posted at least 175 tackles (199), 10 sacks (13.5) and 15 passes defensed (16), and he's the only defensive tackle in NFL history with multiple seasons of 2 or more interceptions, doing it in 2008 and 2014, when he led the team.

Ngata and the Ravens defense

were at their best in the 2014 postseason, allowing just 84 total rushing yards in two games, including an unfathomable 14 yards in a 35–31 loss to the eventual Super Bowl champion Patriots.

It would prove to be Ngata's last hurrah with the Ravens. When the Detroit Lions' Ndamukong Suh signed as a free agent with the Miami Dolphins, the Lions moved to quickly fill the mammoth hole left in the defense by trading two draft picks for Ngata.

"Having Haloti here is a significant addition," says Lions president Tom Lewand. "It means that in a lot of ways we won't

miss a beat. He is a tremendously accomplished player and is a guy that brings a lot more than just his on-the-field presence."

After making a name for himself in the NFL, Ngata started the Haloti Ngata Family Foundation, which helps fight juvenile diabetes, in memory of his mother. His parents couldn't enjoy his professional success, but his first football hero has.

Inside an old journal from childhood, Ngata had tucked away a picture of Moala playing for the University of Utah. On the back it says, "This is my uncle Haloti. He didn't make it to the NFL. But I will."

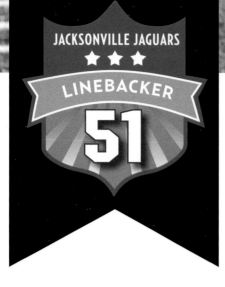

PAUL POSLUSZNY

JACKSONVILLE JAGUARS

★ ★ ★

LINEBACKER

51

It's pronounced "puz-LUZ-nee," but you can call him Poz. Just don't call him late for practice.

"[Paul Posluszny's] a great practice player," said late Penn State coaching legend Joe Paterno. "He's the first one out on the field for practice. He's out there working on shuffling, drops, catching the football. He's everything you want in a college football player."

Posluszny grew up in Aliquippa, Pennsylvania, the same hometown as the New England Patriots star cornerback Darrelle Revis and NFL legends Mike Ditka and Tony Dorsett. At Hopewell High School, he lettered in baseball, basketball and football; on the gridiron he was captain of the 3A state champions in his senior year, dominating on both sides of the ball. He had 88 tackles, six sacks as a linebacker, and set school records with 1,575 rushing yards and 15 touchdowns.

At Penn State, Paterno made Posluszny the first Nittany Lions player since 1968 and 1969 to be named team captain twice. Posluszny also won the Bednarik Award for best defensive player in the country two years in a row and was a First Team All-American in both 2005 and 2006. He added a Butkus Award as the nation's top linebacker, was Division I football Academic All-American of the Year, and was called the "best linebacker to ever play at Penn State" by Hall of Fame linebacker and Penn State alum Jack Ham. There's no higher compliment, considering the school is nicknamed Linebacker U.

The Buffalo Bills drafted Posluszny with the second pick of the second round in 2007. He was the first Bills rookie linebacker to start the season-opening game since 1987. In his first two games he led the Bills in tackles, but injured his forearm in Week 3 and missed 13 games.

Posluszny led his team in tackles in each of the next three seasons, but when his rookie contract expired in 2011, the Jaguars lured him to Jacksonville with a long contract and a more favorable defensive scheme. After his third season in Jacksonville,

he already owned two of the four highest season tackle totals in team history.

Posluszny made the Pro Bowl for the first time in 2013, even though the Jaguars lost their first eight games and ended the season with a 4-12 record. He was second in the NFL with 162 tackles — his sixth straight season with over 100 — and tied for the team lead with two interceptions. He had a career-high three sacks, along with six tackles for loss, two forced fumbles, one fumble recovery and seven quarterback pressures.

IN THE HUDDLE

Posluszny is the first player in NCAA history to record 100-plus tackles in three seasons, and he left Penn State with a school-record 372 tackles.

Posluszny is one of the NFL's elite linebackers, but has the lowest winning percentage of any active NFL player with a minimum of 50 games played. In one of the least telling and most incongruous stats, he's been on a team above .500 for only one game of his career, and his teams have an overall winning percentage hovering around .300.

"You play to win and have success, and when that doesn't happen, it's very frustrating," Posluszny says. "To me, it always cuts deepest when the season is over, your record isn't where you want it to be, and you're watching the playoffs on TV from your couch."

And that was before Posluszny tore his right pectoral in the seventh game of the 2014 season as he sacked Cleveland Browns quarterback Brian Hoyer.

Posluszny already had 12 tackles that day and was on pace to lead the team for the fourth time in his four seasons in Jacksonville. After missing 19 games with the Bills, he'd only missed one as a Jaguar before his pectoral injury.

But unlike many injured players, Poz remained with his teammates and studied video to learn and help when he could.

"What I appreciate is how much he helps those guys [linebackers]," said Jaguars head coach Gus Bradley.

"They turn to him, ask him questions, and he offers insight. It's invaluable, but you can just imagine how it's tearing him up inside."

Posluszny has made a name for himself — not for his career losing percentage but for his leadership, gaudy tackle numbers and relentless pursuit of excellence.

"He's the hardest worker on the team," said former Penn State teammate Dan Connor. "Being the hardest worker and the best player is something you don't see all the time. Sometimes it comes so naturally to great players that they don't feel like they have to work hard. But he works like he's the lowest guy on the food chain trying to work his way up."

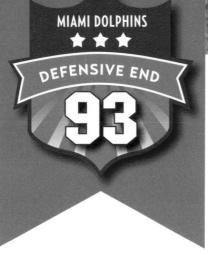

NDAMUKONG SUH

His aggression has earned him a record contract, and his anger has incurred a record fine. At 6-foot-4 and 305 pounds, the man whose name means "house of spears" to Cameroon's Ngemba tribe doesn't tread lightly. Especially not on opponents.

Ndamukong ("en-DOM-ahken") Suh grew up in Portland, Oregon, where he was a prolific soccer player as a kid. He towered over the other players and kicked the ball with such ferocity that his mother, Bernadette, had to carry around his birth certificate to prove he was the same age as his opponents.

With his size, football was inevitable. After dominating on his high school's offensive and defensive lines, Suh went to the University of Nebraska. He became a Cornhusker legend by winning just about every defensive award and finishing fourth in Heisman voting as a senior — a rarity for a lineman.

The Detroit Lions took Suh with the second overall pick in the 2010 draft, and in his first season he had 10 sacks, won the Defensive Rookie of the Year Award and was named to the Pro Bowl and All-Pro teams. He also

opened his account with the league's disciplinary committee, incurring some hefty fines for dirty play.

"The problem with the league is they've never seen a defensive tackle like this," explained Detroit's defensive coordinator Gunther Cunningham. "He's the best football player at that position I've ever seen."

In just one season, Suh became the face of the Lions' defense, and, by helping replace a local high school football team's equipment after it was stolen, a public figure in Detroit.

IN THE HUDDLE

In 2014, Suh led the Lions in sacks with 8.5 and became the Lions' all-time sack leader as a defensive tackle. He also had a career-high 21 tackles for loss, passing Hall of Famer Warren Sapp for the most by a defensive tackle since 2000.

"To have a positive role model like Ndamukong Suh come to our city — I'm excited about the young people who will be impacted by his success," said Tyrone Winfrey, president of the Detroit Board of Education.

Therein lies the dichotomy of Suh: he engenders goodwill and respect off the field, yet on it he has been known to cross the line. In the traditional Thanksgiving Day game between the Lions and the Green Bay Packers in 2011, Suh shoved Packers guard Evan Dietrich-Smith's head into the turf after the play was over and then stomped on his arm for good measure.

After the game, Suh said he was simply trying to catch his balance, but the league didn't buy it, and he was suspended for two games without pay.

In September, Suh topped a survey by Nielsen and E-Poll Market Research as the most liked NFL player. A mere three months later in a poll published in *Forbes*, he was voted one of the most disliked athletes in America.

Suh eventually apologized for his actions. "Playing professional sports is not a game," he wrote on his Facebook page. "It is a profession with great responsibility, and where performance on and off the field should never be compromised. It requires a calm and determined demeanor, which cannot be derailed by the game, referee calls, fans or other players."

When the temperature and stakes rise, Suh isn't quite as measured. He successfully appealed a suspension that would have kept him out of a 2014 playoff game against the Dallas Cowboys after another stomp — this time on Packers quarterback Aaron Rodgers.

The one-game suspension was reduced to a $70,000 fine, the ninth of Suh's career. These included one for $30,000 for kicking then Houston Texans quarterback Matt Schaub in the groin and a record-setting $100,000 for a low block in 2013. But the $286,875 he's

CAREER HIGHLIGHTS

- Three-time First Team All-Pro selection (2010, 2013–14)
- Second Team All-Pro (2012)
- Four-time Pro Bowl selection (2010, 2012–14)
- Defensive Rookie of the Year (2010)
- Unanimous All-America selection (2009)

paid the NFL won't cost him too much sleep: he decided to take his talents to South Beach as a free agent and signed the richest defensive contract in NFL history.

"I was never looking to want to leave and figure out a different situation," Suh told the *Detroit Free Press* about his six-year, $114 million Miami contract. "But at the end of the day, I have to do what's best for myself and for my family."

"He'll do well for them; he is an outstanding player," says an unnamed Lions management source. "But Miami better quickly learn to understand the product and the person they have. And that part of it, I assure you, will not be easy."

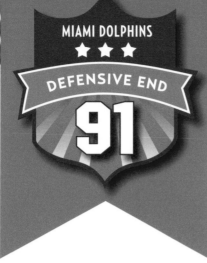

CAMERON WAKE

At 6-foot-3 and 262 pounds, Cameron Wake is a little too small to stand out on an NFL field. Among the khakis and cubicles of Maryland's Castle Point Mortgage, however, he was a bit more conspicuous. He was also named Derek then.

Wake's circuitous route to NFL stardom started in Hyattsville, Maryland, where he didn't play football until his junior year of high school, turning to the sport after being cut from the basketball team. His strength and speed made up for his late start and earned him a scholarship to Penn State.

Wake was good enough to start games for the Nittany Lions all four of his years there, mostly at linebacker but occasionally at defensive end. He finished with 191 total tackles, two forced fumbles, 8.5 sacks, 24 tackles for loss and seven blocked kicks, but he wasn't good enough to be drafted into the NFL. Despite eye-popping scouting combine numbers, including a 45.5-inch vertical leap — the highest that's ever been recorded at the event — scouts couldn't see past his size.

After a failed free agent tryout with the New York Giants, Wake went to work selling mortgages over the phone in suburban Maryland. He sat at a desk for eight hours a day but also spent four more in the gym.

Wake still had the football itch, and mortgages weren't scratching it, so he quit his job to work — and work out — full time at his gym. It was where he started to go by Cameron, his middle name. His coworkers thought Cameron was his first name because of a paperwork error, and he thought the name represented a new start.

The new Cameron Wake got a shot at pro football with the Canadian Football League's BC Lions.

IN THE HUDDLE

After six seasons Wake is fifth in Dolphins history with 63.0 sacks, and seventh in NFL history among undrafted players.

Wake brought the bare minimum with him and living in a basement apartment, he focused on the business of football, eschewing technology and the nightlife of his new city.

It paid off handsomely.

In 2007, Wake was named both Rookie of the Year and Most Outstanding Defensive Player — the only player in CFL history to win both in the same season. He defended the latter in his second year.

Being light and quick, by defensive end standards, works in the CFL because the field is wider and the quarterbacks tend to be more mobile. As a result, Wake had 16 and 23 sacks, respectively, in his two seasons.

Suddenly, Wake was NFL worthy, with nine teams fighting for his services. The Miami Dolphins won the bidding war, signing him to a four-year contract worth almost $5 million in 2009.

Wake started fast, making a tackle on the opening kickoff of the first game of his NFL career in 2009, and in 2010 he started every game of the season as a linebacker and finished third in the league with

14.0 sacks. He was a Second Team All-Pro, was selected for the Pro Bowl and was voted by his peers as one of the NFL Network's Top 100 players.

In 2012, Wake moved to defensive end, and his 15.0 sacks were fourth in the league and a new career high. He also had 53 tackles and three forced fumbles, and was honored with his first appearance on the All-Pro First Team.

When Wake's not racking up sack totals, he's wreaking havoc with quarterback hits, hurries and pressures — less sexy stats but game-changing ones. In 2014 he had 11.5 sacks, good for 11th in the NFL, and he made his third All-Pro team and fourth Pro Bowl appearance.

A young 32, thanks to his three-year football hiatus, Wake still relies on his speed to get to the quarterback. He also has an uncanny knack for running full speed while his upper body is parallel to the ground. His style of play is built for today's NFL, as it was for the CFL: going under and around the offensive line to track down agile quarterbacks.

Wake keeps one bacteria-soaked

CAREER HIGHLIGHTS

- First Team All-Pro (2012)

- Two-time Second Team All-Pro selection (2010, 2014)

- Four-time Pro Bowl selection (2010, 2012–14)

- Two-time CFL Most Outstanding Defensive Player (2007–08)

- CFL Rookie of the Year (2007)

reminder of his days in Canada: the shower shoes emblazoned with the CFL logo that he was issued on day one of Lions training camp. He still wears them at the Dolphins facility.

"The sandals are a simple reminder never to get complacent, always be humble; that I was a guy with a three-figure bank account, bought clothes from a thrift store," says Derek Cameron Wake.

"It's not where you start, it's where you finish. Whatever's made me into me, I'm not too upset about it."

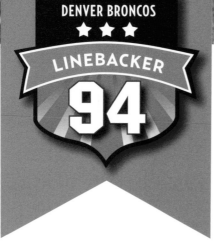

DeMARCUS WARE

DENVER BRONCOS
★ ★ ★
LINEBACKER
94

As a teenager, DeMarcus Ware made extra cash hawking soft drinks in the stands at Auburn Tigers football games. He was a high school football standout, and dreamt of being at the university stadium in a Tigers uniform, not a vendor bib.

During his years at Auburn High School in Alabama, Ware was a four-sport star, excelling at basketball, baseball, track and football. It was on the gridiron, however, where he really shone, earning nods as most valuable linebacker and wide receiver while playing alongside future All-Pro and Pro Bowl linebacker Osi Umenyiora.

But Ware's dream didn't come true; he wouldn't be a Tiger. Instead, he ended up at the only college that recruited him — Alabama's Troy University. Success took a few years, but as a senior, Ware was named a Third Team All-American, All–Sun Belt and Sun Belt Defensive Player of the Year. He finished with 53 tackles, 29 pressures and 19 tackles for loss, as well as a career-high 10.5 sacks and 4 forced fumbles to lead the Trojans to their first bowl appearance.

Even with these accolades, Ware was seen as a "tweener" when he entered the 2005 draft, falling somewhere between a defensive end and an outside linebacker. Projected to go in the second round, Cowboys owner Jerry Jones had a little more faith in Ware and insisted Dallas take him in the first round with the 11th overall pick.

Foresight is what made Jones a billionaire, and his projection that selecting Ware early in the draft would pay off was an astute one. In just four years Ware became one of the league's most explosive and dominant defenders. Overall, he's had double-digit sack totals in eight of his 10 seasons, including an NFL-best mark of 20 in 2008 and 15.5 in 2010, making him just the fifth player to top the league more than once.

While building this impressive résumé and fearsome reputation, Ware was also dealing with emotionally crippling challenges off the field. He and his wife, Taniqua, suffered three failed pregnancies, which included their son Omar, who was stillborn.

IN THE HUDDLE

Ware was the second-quickest player, behind Reggie White, to reach 100 career sacks, doing it in 113 games, and he's 14th in career sacks in NFL history with 127.0.

Omar's memory is Ware's inspiration. "I feel Omar out there with me, watching over me and protecting me. Sometimes, when I'm tired on the field, and I feel like I can't go anymore, I just think, what if he had one more breath? What if all three did?"

The Wares were blessed with three children — two adopted and one biological — before they divorced in 2012.

DeMarcus, however, has become all too familiar with conscious uncoupling: in 2014 the Cowboys decided they too

should part ways with the talented linebacker. Despite the fact that he set five of the top-6 sack totals in Cowboys history, and was both in the Pro Bowl and an All-Pro seven out of nine years in Dallas, the Cowboys released him after an injury-filled 2013 season.

For owner Jones, Ware's cap hit was too high for the Cowboys, and the linebacker wasn't interested in taking a pay cut to stay with the team. At that point, letting Ware go was purely a shrewd business decision, and Ware hit the free agent market prior to the 2014 season.

The Denver Broncos believed in Ware's powers of recovery. Needing a defensive upgrade after being humiliated in Super Bowl XLVII, Ware was someone Denver believed could fill the dual role of on-field difference maker and mentor to blossoming superstar linebacker Von Miller. A three-year, $30 million deal later, the project was given the green light.

In his first season with the Broncos at the age of 32, Ware played all 16 games, had 10.0 sacks and made it back to the Pro Bowl for the eighth time.

"All he needed [was to] get healthy," says Denver teammate C.J. Anderson. "You are talking about a Hall of Famer, one of the best of all time."

He's not a Hall of Famer quite yet, but his career arc looks promising. Ware is still active and elite, and he's taken the advice of current Hall of Famer Michael Strahan, who stressed to Ware the upside of being lighter and leaner in the later stages of his career. And Ware is constantly learning and refining moves he picks up from legends of the line and young stars alike — that is, when he's not pioneering his own.

Ware used a heady mix of veteran savvy and speed to put a double-spin move on San Francisco 49ers Pro Bowl offensive tackle Joe Staley and to sack Colin Kaepernick, arguably the fastest

CAREER HIGHLIGHTS

- Eight-time Pro Bowl selection (2006–12, 2014)
- Four-time First Team All-Pro selection (2007–09, 2011)
- Three-time Second Team All-Pro selection (2006, 2010, 2012)
- Two-time NFL sack leader (2008, 2010)
- NFC Defensive Player of the Year (2008)
- NFL 2000s All-Decade Team

quarterback in the league. It was part of a three-sack night during the Broncos sixth game of the season. It was also a rare instance of a lineman going viral.

"Nothing about him surprises me," former Denver coach John Fox said after coaching Ware for a year. "He's had an incredible career."

J.J. WATT

A kid playing sports and clamoring for the right to wear number 99 isn't a new phenomenon; it's just always been associated with hockey ever since Wayne Gretzky rewrote the NHL record book in the 1980s and 90s. Now, Justin James "J.J." Watt, who grew up playing hockey in Wisconsin, has a generation of young football players fighting for the number when the jerseys are handed out in the fall.

Watt played elite-level hockey against a handful of future NHL players until the age of 13, when his parents, Connie and John, decided the money and travel for him and his two younger brothers was too much.

Hockey's loss was football's gain, even if he was scrawny and awkward until well into his time at Pewaukee High. There, Watt started as a 5-foot-9 freshman quarterback who grew to be 6-foot-2 by his junior year, and who even then was still "all knees and elbows," according to coach Clay Iverson.

But Watt was determined and still growing. As a senior he was a defensive end and tight end, earning a scholarship to Central Michigan University on offense. He played one season there but didn't feel tight end was the right position for him, and decided to go home and try his luck as a walk-on at the University of Wisconsin.

Watt earned a scholarship after beating up the starting offensive linemen as a member of the scout team, and went on to start 26 games at strong-side defensive end. He recorded 106 tackles, 11.5 sacks and 36.5 stops for losses of 144 yards, as well as 28 quarterback pressures. He also recovered four fumbles and caused four others, blocked four kicks and deflected 13 passes. His stellar all-around play earned him a First Team All-America selection by the NFL Draft Report.

IN THE HUDDLE

Watt is the first player in NFL history with three touchdown catches, an interception return for a touchdown and a fumble return for a touchdown in one season — one more touchdown catch than Jay Arnold had in 1938. Watt is also the first defensive player since 1948 to have four touchdowns in a season.

"[J.J. Watt is a] player who gets it and has gotten it for a long time. He has surrounded himself with good people and has a level head. He could be a star on the field and then a governor once his career ends," read one scouting report of Watt.

With a few extra inches and a filled-out frame, the 6-foot-5 and 289 pound defensive end was drafted by the Houston Texans 11th overall in 2011, and in his first season he helped the team go from 30th in the league in team defense to second.

He also had 3.5 sacks and an interception return for a touchdown in two playoff games — making him known to fans league-wide.

In 2012, Watt truly emerged. In just his second season he had 39 tackles for loss, led the NFL with 20.5 sacks and was named Defensive Player of the Year. Prior to the 2014 season, he signed what was the richest contract for a defensive player in NFL history — a six-year, $100 million extension. He was up before dawn that day working out, already concerned he wouldn't live up to it.

He did and then some. Watt had 20.5 sacks again, an interception, which he returned 80 yards for a touchdown, five fumble recoveries (one for a touchdown), a safety and 78 tackles. Just for fun — and because he can — he also caught three passes for four yards and three touchdowns.

Watt was named Defensive Player of the Year for the second time in three seasons in 2014, but this time it was unanimous — the first time in history a defensive player had taken every vote.

Ascending to the top of America's most popular sport does have its drawbacks. Watt's neighbours requested he stop handing out candy at Halloween because of the traffic, and he hires an assistant to buy his groceries — not because he can't do it himself, but because his good nature would have him talking with fans all day. Despite these sacrifices, as well as his television cameos on *The League* and his A-list celebrity friends, Watt remains down-to-earth. He lives modestly despite his monster contract, and he visits Houston hospitals anonymously — for as long as he can keep his identity under wraps.

He also continues to play hard. Watt is notorious for playing as if the next down were his last. The salient image of blood pouring from the bridge of his nose from a wound he keeps reopening is like a throwback to the NFL's more gladiatorial days. He looks as though he were put on the field by central casting, plays as though he were built in a lab, and is generally regarded as one of the sport's good guys.

He is, in the words of former Texans coach Wade Phillips, "the perfect football player."

MARIO WILLIAMS

When Mario Williams was growing up, he idolized Barry Sanders and Emmitt Smith and dreamt of being an NFL running back. When fully grown to a chiseled 6-foot-6 and 285 pounds, genetics dictated that he become a legend at dishing out punishment — not taking it.

"It looks like Mario Williams has baby seals connecting his shoulders to his elbows," *Muscle &* *Fitness* once commented.

Williams can bench-press 450 pounds, has a 41-inch vertical leap and has enough speed to run the ball if he really wants to. At Richlands High School in North Carolina, he had 590 yards rushing on only 58 carries, but it was his 87 tackles (including 22 for a loss) and 13 sacks in his senior year that earned him a scholarship to North Carolina State University.

Most of North Carolina's defensive record book was dismantled by Williams in his three years with the Wolfpack, including stops for loss in a career (55.5) and season (27.5), and sacks in a career (26.5) and season (14.5). After his junior year, he was named a First Team All-American by TheDraftReport.com and *Sports Illustrated,* and he declared for the 2006 NFL draft.

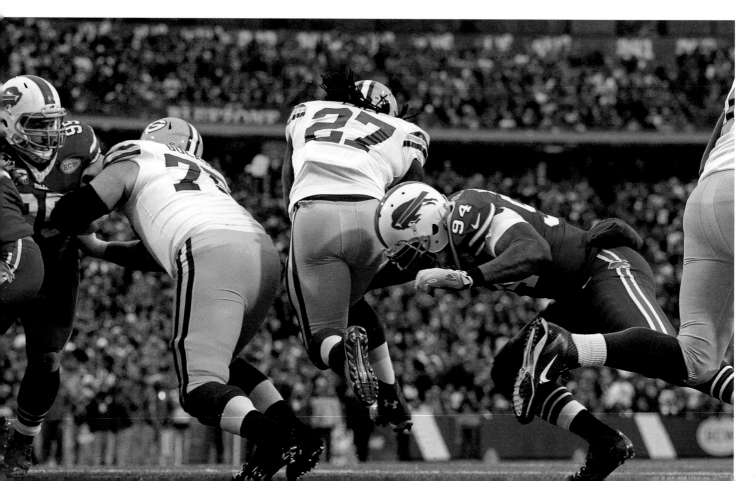

That year many were shocked when the Texans, only four seasons into their existence and with a losing record in each one, didn't pick the biggest name on the board: Heisman winner and college legend Reggie Bush, then a tailback at the University of Southern California. Instead, the Texans drafted Williams first overall.

IN THE HUDDLE

After just four seasons, Williams held the Texans' franchise record for career sacks; he currently sits at 53.0 for his career.

Assessing the situation, ESPN.com writer Len Pasquarelli wrote, "Ladies and gentlemen, your Houston Texans, an outfit that might do better were Mr. Magoo executing its lottery selections."

The Texans weren't blind. Williams went on to set Houston's single-season team sack record in 2007 with 14.0. His first sack was against then Indianapolis Colts quarterback Peyton Manning, a superstar and division rival the Texans drafted Williams to stop. At one point late in the season, Williams had 55 total tackles (including sacks, unassisted tackles and assisted tackles) and of those 55 plays, opponents gained a total of 1.5 yards — 0.02 yards per play.

Williams followed up 2007 with 12 sacks in 2008 and 9 in 2009, numbers that led the team and got Williams voted into the Pro Bowl twice. In 2010 he missed games for the first time in his career because of a sports hernia, and in 2011, Williams tore his pectoral muscle and was lost for the remainder of the year.

After his shortened season, the Texans weren't willing to break the bank to keep Williams around, and the Buffalo Bills swooped in and signed Williams to a six-year, incentive-laden deal that could land the hulking defensive end up to $100 million.

In three seasons in Buffalo, Williams has earned his paycheck. He's missed only one game and has recorded double-digit sacks in each season. And his ninth year in the league, normally when pass rushers are limping towards retirement, was one of his best.

The 2014 season was memorable on and off the field. Williams won AFC Defensive Player of the Month in November, set a new career high with 14.5 sacks, was named a First Team All-Pro for the second time and played in his fourth Pro Bowl. His career marks after the season included 90 sacks, 367 tackles and 16 forced fumbles. And Buffalo is now an adopted city full of grateful residents.

Williams plowed his way into the hearts of Buffalonians by clearing snow from city streets after a historic storm dumped six feet of snow and paralyzed the city. Afterwards, he helped deliver breakfast to snowbound locals, cruising in his Caterpillar plow, wearing a Bills helmet and blasting "Eye of the Tiger" from the speakers.

Documenting his snow removal on social media, Williams' hashtags were apt for both that morning and his defensive career: #neverbreakcharacter and #mrdelivery.

DEFENSIVE BACKS

CLEVELAND BROWNS

CORNERBACK

23

JOE HADEN

CAREER HIGHLIGHTS

- Two-time Pro Bowl selection (2013–14)
- Second Team All-Pro (2013)
- Unanimous First Team All-America selection and a finalist for the Jim Thorpe Award (2009)

Joseph Walter Haden III, who has four younger brothers — Jordan, Jonathon, Jacob and Josh — set a Maryland public school record with 7,371 career passing yards and tied the career mark for touchdown passes with 80 while playing at Fort Washington's Friendly High School. As a senior he threw for 2,783 yards and 38 touchdowns, rushed for 899 yards and 13 touchdowns, and won the Class 3A state title with a 14-0 record. He was also a starter on the school's state-winning basketball team.

After graduating early and enrolling at the University of Florida in January 2007, Haden switched positions twice (from quarterback to wide receiver to defensive back) before becoming the first true freshman in University of Florida history to start at cornerback in his first career game. At season's end he was a freshman All-American.

After being named a First Team All-American in his junior year, he declared for the 2010 draft and was taken with the seventh overall pick by the Cleveland Browns.

Success followed Haden to the NFL too. As a rookie in 2010 he played all 16 games and led the Browns with 18 passes broken up and six interceptions, including one in four straight games — the first Brown since 1968 to do that.

In 2011, Cleveland was second in the league in pass defense, their highest ranking since 1962. Haden led the team with 19 passes defensed, to go with 65 tackles, a sack, a fumble recovery and a forced fumble.

IN THE HUDDLE

Haden owns over 1,200 pairs of shoes and co-owns Restock, a consignment store in downtown Cleveland that specializes in rare and vintage sneakers.

His star having risen, Haden became a man about Cleveland, often appearing at Cavaliers and Indians games, but the bon vivant lifestyle caught up with him. In 2012 he received a four-game suspension after testing positive for the banned stimulant Adderall. It wasn't ingested to enhance football performance; the stimulant was available at a party in Las Vegas during the off-season.

While serving his suspension, Haden got engaged to girlfriend Sarah Mahmoodshahi, whom he married in 2013. In his absence the Browns went 0-4, giving up 10 touchdown passes when they'd only allowed 16 during the entire 2011 season. They were 26th in the league in pass defense, after being second the year prior.

Haden didn't deny taking the

drug, but the time-out changed him. "I was living the lifestyle, having a ball. But the suspension showed just how quickly everything can be taken away from you. It was just an overall feeling of 'I'm getting older. I have a great woman.' I proposed and got serious with my religion. It was time to grow up."

Haden has defended more passes than anyone in the NFL since he joined the league, and in 2014 the Browns gave him a five-year, $67.5 million contract extension. One of the first things he did after signing was provide 40,000 meals for families in Northeast Ohio through the Greater Cleveland Food Bank. In 2015 he also became the first NFL player named a Special Olympics Global Ambassador, representing an event his brother Jacob has

participated in.

Expectations were high with the new contract in hand and having been voted 39th on NFL.com's annual list of the league's top-100 players in 2014, just two spots behind cornerback legend Darrelle Revis. But Haden had a rough start to the season. The lowlight was when receiver Steve Smith Sr. beat him with the game on the line in a heartbreaking 23–21 loss to the Baltimore Ravens. Twitter was swift and harsh, with writer Matt Miller of Bleacher Report calling him "overrated" — one of the bigger insults in sports.

When all was said and done, however, Haden had 73 tackles and three interceptions in 2014, and he received All-Pro votes and was named to the Pro Bowl for the

second consecutive year.

"I think his salary says it all," says Ravens wide receiver Torrey Smith, a childhood friend. "If people from the outside don't want to respect it, his organization does — as they should. Going against him twice a year, every year, I definitely think you can put him out there anytime and argue with anyone as [to his] being the best in the league."

The Browns haven't made the playoffs since 2002 and haven't won a playoff game since 1994, but long-suffering Cleveland fans know patience. With the return of LeBron James to the NBA's Cavaliers and the emergence of Haden as a marquee NFL player, they now have two superstars in town wearing number 23, and they have hope. Now they just need their storybook ending.

PATRICK PETERSON

There's football talent in Patrick Peterson's bloodlines — four cousins, two on each side of the family, have played in the NFL — and his skill was nurtured from an early age.

Patrick Sr. taught his young son to return punts, starting with the catch. The lesson was to use his hands, not his body, and he lobbed tennis balls, golf balls and water balloons to make his point and soften his son's hands. Those adventures in catching and returning wouldn't pay off for a while, since coaches in youth football rarely call for a punt on fourth down. And, after scoring four touchdowns against the defending champions as a six-year-old, Peterson was disqualified from his kids team — for being too *young* to play.

His father taught him another important lesson in his sophomore year at Blanche Ely High School in Pompano Beach, Florida. Football always came easy to Peterson, but Dad, who was also head coach, kicked him off the team because of poor grades.

"It was a jaw-dropping moment, but it definitely helped me put a lot of things in perspective," says Peterson. "It helped me be a better player and a better person."

With his academics and priorities in order, Peterson

was named the USA TODAY Defensive Player of the Year in his senior year of high school, while also tacking on 733 yards rushing and 11 touchdowns on offense.

As a junior at Louisiana State in 2010, the 6-foot-1, 219-pound Peterson won both the Bednarik Award as the nation's top defender — the first defensive back to win since Charles Woodson in 1997 — and the Thorpe Award as the country's top defensive back. He was the first LSU player to win either award, and he was a unanimous All-American. With little left to prove, he skipped his senior season and declared for the 2011 draft.

IN THE HUDDLE

Only six players in NFL history have returned a punt 80-plus yards for a touchdown at least four times in their career. Peterson did it in his first 31 career returns.

If Peterson's pedigree and collegiate accolades weren't impressive enough, his performance at the NFL scouting combine cemented his reputation as a can't-miss prospect. His numbers were otherworldly: a 38-inch vertical leap, a 10-foot-6 broad jump, a 4.31-second 40-yard dash, a 4.07-second 20-yard shuttle run, an 11.01-second 60-yard shuttle run and a 6.58-second three-cone drill.

The Arizona Cardinals made Peterson the first cornerback taken in the draft when they selected him fifth overall, and his father's lessons finally paid off, in a big way.

Peterson set a rookie record and led the NFL with 699 punt return yards, the second highest in NFL history. He also scored four touchdowns off punt returns to become only the fourth player

in history with as many punt return TDs in a single season, tying the NFL record. He was just the second rookie with four, after the Detroit Lions' Jack Christiansen in 1951. With scoring returns of 99, 89, 82 and 80 yards, he was the first player in history with four punt return touchdowns of 80-plus yards in a single season.

In four NFL seasons Peterson hasn't missed a game, and he's been in the Pro Bowl every year, the first as a kick returner and the last three as a cornerback. He's also been a First Team All-Pro at two different positions — kick returner in 2011 and cornerback in 2013.

A multipurpose weapon like Peterson is a golden ticket, and with a five-year, $70 million extension prior to the 2014 season, the Cardinals ensured he would stick around. Peterson's contract topped the one signed two months prior by Richard Sherman, his competition for best cornerback in the league. The two have a social media beef going — sometimes good-natured, sometimes bitter — but one general manager who wished to remain anonymous rates Peterson higher.

"[Peterson] is big, tough and lines up all over the place. He can play the press-man you want, and he takes the other team's best receiver. He can go into the slot. He can go to the left side, the right side. It doesn't matter. That's the difference. I don't think you could put Sherman in their scheme and [have him] do the same things."

Peterson's versatility also tips the scales. In a 2013 game against the Lions, he was the first defensive player since at least 1970 to have a reception and a completion in a game. After the game, his gloves and the ball were sent to the Hall of Fame in Canton. When his career is over, his bust and induction will likely be close behind.

CAREER HIGHLIGHTS

• Two-time First Team All-Pro selection (2011, 2013)

• Four-time Pro Bowl selection (2011–14)

• Led the NFL and set a rookie record with 699 punt return yards (2011)

• Bednarik Award and Thorpe Award winner (2010)

DARRELLE REVIS

NEW YORK JETS

CORNERBACK 24

You can go home again. New York versus New England is one of sports' most heated regional rivalries. And while New Yorkers won't like the fact that Darrelle Revis had to go to New England to win a Super Bowl, Jets fans will be ready to forgive the All-Pro cornerback if he can help save a stumbling team.

New York is where Revis made a name — and nickname — for himself. Rikers Island is a notorious prison where the city's hardened criminals go for a time-out; residents of "Revis Island" are the NFL's best receivers, stranded by the

5-foot-11, 198-pound shutdown cornerback with the impressive agility, speed, vision and instincts.

Growing up in Aliquippa, Pennsylvania, inside a 13-room home where four generations of his family lived together, Revis could see past the rundown rows of houses to the bleachers of Aliquippa High School. That's where the whole town gathered on Friday nights to watch the football team. It's the field he'd own as a quarterback, wide receiver, defensive back and kick returner. In his senior year in 2003 he was named Pennsylvania Player of the Year.

Revis attended the University of Pittsburgh, where he focused on defense and completed a three-year career with 129 tackles, 8 interceptions and 4 touchdowns (two from interceptions and two on punt returns) before skipping his senior season to enter the NFL draft. The Jets chose Revis 14th overall in 2007 after trading first-, second- and fifth-round draft picks to the Carolina Panthers in order to move up and draft him one spot ahead of his hometown Pittsburgh Steelers.

The Jets knew they were getting an elite cornerback;

CAREER HIGHLIGHTS

- Six-time Pro Bowl selection (2008–2011, 2013–14)

- Four-time First Team All-Pro selection (2009–2011, 2014)

- AFC Defensive Player of the Year (2009)

- All-Rookie Team (2007)

they also got a workaholic. Revis obsessively studies film, learning the tendencies and tells of the receivers he will face. He takes this a step further by tailoring specific workouts to combat his opponents. "He just attacks his job," said former Jets coach Rex Ryan. "If there is one guy I want to cover somebody, with my paycheck on it, I want it to be Darrelle Revis."

IN THE HUDDLE

Revis is the 22nd-highest-earning player in NFL history and the sixth-highest-earning defensive player. If he plays out his full contract, he'll have earned over $150 million, making him the highest-paid defensive player of all time.

In 2009 and 2010 Revis was a First Team All-Pro, and the Jets made two straight trips to the AFC Championship Game, both losses. Prior to the 2011 season, ESPN graded and ranked every player in the NFL; Revis was tied at the top with quarterbacks Tom Brady and Peyton Manning and running back Adrian Peterson. Revis lived up to expectations in 2011 with 52 tackles, 21 passes defensed and 4 interceptions, including one he returned 100 yards for a touchdown against the Miami Dolphins. The Jets stumbled though and missed the playoffs with an 8-8 record.

Revis admits the Jets were in "disarray" in 2011, and it went downhill from there in 2012. During another desultory season for the team, he tore his ACL in the fifth game and was out for the remainder of the year.

Faced with both Revis' reconstructed knee and restructuring his contract, the Jets traded him to the Tampa Bay Buccaneers for the 13th overall pick in the 2013 draft.

Revis signed a six-year, $96 million contract with the Bucs, which made him the highest-paid defensive back in NFL history. He lasted only a season in the NFL

wilderness of Tampa Bay, playing all 16 games and making the Pro Bowl. But Tampa decided to release their splashy acquisition instead of paying him the big-money bonus he was due.

The New England Patriots signed Revis hours later, and he was back in the spotlight with the perennial contenders. They hadn't won a Super Bowl in a decade and had been shopping for a shutdown cornerback most of that time. Revis was named a First Team All-Pro for the fourth time in his career in 2014, and he made impact plays in the playoffs, intercepting Andrew Luck in the AFC Championship Game and sacking Russell Wilson in the Patriots' 28–24 Super Bowl XLIX

victory over the Seattle Seahawks.

But the Patriots aren't a team burdened by loyalty, especially to players over 30. They released Revis, who then signed a five-year, $70 million contract — $39 million guaranteed — with the Jets.

"It was a no-brainer to come here because I know the organization," said Revis of returning to New York and reviving Revis Island. "They drafted me and I have a lot of history here . . . This is where my heart is."

And maybe, with the wisdom of roads traveled and a championship pedigree, Revis can bring some much-needed respectability back to the Jets, and let the fans dream of a long-awaited second Super Bowl title, 47 years after their last.

RICHARD SHERMAN

"U mad bro?"

Posted after a game in the early part of the 2012 season, the tweet made Richard Sherman a social media star and garnered him thousands of followers and nearly as many enemies. On the field, he and the Seattle Seahawks were carving a very similar path.

At the time of the tweet, the Seahawks were coming off a 7-9 season, and Sherman was a young player with little profile beyond the Pacific Northwest. The New England Patriots were defending AFC champions and were winning 23–10 in the fourth quarter of their Week 6 matchup. But rookie quarterback Russell Wilson sparked an improbable comeback win, and Sherman, who had been nipping at quarterback Tom Brady's heels all day, escorted him off the field to rub it in. It was then a picture was taken that Sherman later retweeted with the infamous caption.

Brash and cocky, yes, but there's more to Sherman than a bit of trash-talk text. He grew up in Compton, California — usually a dead end of gang life and crime for most kids. But he had a 4.2 GPA at Dominguez High School, while also starring in football and track and field. He was also learning to combine the power of elite athletic talent with a sharp mind — as his hero, Muhammad Ali, had — while also emulating the verbal barrages of neighborhood rappers turned cultural icons.

Sherman could've attended local football powerhouse USC, but he chose to become the first athlete in more than 20 years to go to Stanford based on both academic and athletic qualifications. A receiver for three seasons, he became a cornerback in his senior year after clashing with coach Jim Harbaugh. He had modest receiving totals, but his defense was great, with 112 tackles and six interceptions. He also ran the 100-meter hurdles and did long jump and triple jump for Stanford. He graduated with a 3.9 GPA and a degree in communications.

Drafted in the fifth round by

CAREER HIGHLIGHTS

- Three-time First Team All-Pro selection (2012–14)

- Two-time Pro Bowl selection (2013–14)

- Led the NFL in interceptions, with 8 (2013)

- ESPY Award for Best Breakthrough Athlete (2014)

the Seahawks in 2011, Sherman says he can still name every cornerback picked before him that year, and none have had his success. He's been a First Team All-Pro for three consecutive seasons (2012–14) and is the leader of the league's most dominating defense. Over the 2013 and 2014 seasons, Seattle's "Legion of Boom" backfield has allowed the league's fewest completions, yards and touchdowns.

IN THE HUDDLE
Since Sherman was drafted in 2011, he's had the most interceptions in the NFL (24), nine more than anyone else.

In the 2013 NFC title game against the San Francisco 49ers, Sherman tipped a pass intended for Michael Crabtree in the end zone, which linebacker Malcolm Smith intercepted. It sealed the game and sent the Seahawks to the Super Bowl. After the play, Sherman extended a hand to Crabtree, who pushed him away. Sherman insists his gesture was genuine.

Immediately following the game, sideline reporter Erin Andrews interviewed an emotional Sherman, who said, "I'm the best corner in the game. When you try me with a sorry receiver like Crabtree, that's the result you're going to get. Don't you ever talk about me."

Asked whom he was referring to, Sherman replied, "Crabtree. Don't you open your mouth about the best, or I'll shut it for you real quick."

The rant, based as much on the preceding play as it was on a slight from Crabtree months prior that Sherman had filed away, became fodder for media far beyond the football beat. Sherman was vilified as a "thug." It was a lazy insult based on his hometown and dreadlocks and one that ignored his Stanford degree. The criticism itself led to another round of social dissection

among the chattering classes.

And Sherman was right about being the best cornerback in the game. He led the league in 2013 with eight interceptions, and the Seahawks won Super Bowl XLVIII in dominant fashion, beating the Denver Broncos 43–8, even with Sherman hobbled by an ankle injury.

A year later in the 2014 playoffs, Sherman had an athletic end-zone interception in the Seahawks come-from-behind victory against the Green Bay Packers in the NFC title game. He played Super Bowl XLIX against the New England Patriots with a torn ulnar collateral ligament in his left elbow, which he sustained in the NFC title game. But the tables were turned on Seattle. Unheralded Patriots cornerback Malcolm Butler was the star, intercepting a pass on the goal line with less than 30 seconds left to clinch New England's 28–24 victory.

Sherman wrote just before

the Super Bowl that he planned to be a role model for the son he and girlfriend Ashley Moss were expecting. Rayden Sherman eased the pain of the loss by arriving days later, fittingly on February 5th — 2/5 for No. 25.

Just one year removed from the Crabtree incident, Sherman showed he had grown and could lose with class. As the clock struck zero on the Seahawks' Super Bowl defeat, Sherman reached out his hand in congratulations to Brady, who was still kneeling down and cradling the ball. A picture of the moment became a defining image of the most watched TV event in American history.

It appears Brady is ignoring him in that split second, but after the shutter clicked, Brady stood up and shook hands with Sherman — two of the biggest stars in football coming together in mutual respect and sportsmanship.

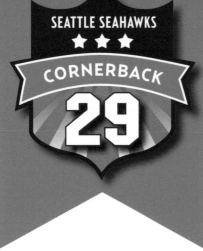

EARL THOMAS

In 1987, Debbie Thomas was diagnosed with cervical cancer and told she had six months to live. Two months later the cancer had inexplicably disappeared, and two years after that she gave birth to Earl Thomas III, her "miracle child."

Earl III grew up in Orange, Texas, where grandfather Earl built a church and became the pastor, and where father Earl taught him and his brother, Seth, to tackle in the garage. When he was a junior at West Orange-Stark High School, the town was devastated by Hurricane Rita. His family escaped unscathed, but their house was destroyed, and they were forced to live in a Motel 6 before the Federal Emergency Management Agency (FEMA) provided a mobile home.

Undeterred by motel life and a diet almost exclusively composed of Waffle House fare, Thomas was unstoppable during his senior year. He played defensive back, running back and wide receiver, and finished his high school career with 112 tackles, 11 interceptions, two kickoff return touchdowns and two punt return touchdowns, to go with 1,850 yards rushing and 2,140 receiving.

Thomas then left Orange to wear orange with the University of Texas, but not until his second year in Austin. At 5-foot-10 and 174 pounds, he was deemed too small

to be a safety and was redshirted his first season. Sitting out the year gave him time to learn the cornerback position and bulk up to over 200 pounds, and in 2008 he was a First Team Freshman All-American. As a sophomore he was a Consensus All-American for the 13-0 Longhorns, whose only loss of the season was in the national title game to the University of Alabama.

IN THE HUDDLE

In 2013, Thomas became the first safety in a decade to have 100-plus tackles, 5-plus interceptions and 2-plus forced fumbles in a single season.

With two years played and three removed from high school (because of his redshirt season), Thomas was eligible for the 2010 draft and chose to enter so he could take care of his family. He was chosen with the 14th overall pick by new coach Pete Carroll and the Seattle Seahawks.

Thomas wasn't an immediate success. He relied more on talent and instinct than positioning in his first NFL season, and admits he might not have been the best teammate. But with some maturation off the field and with help from secondary coach Kris Richard, he had 98 tackles and two interceptions in 2011, earning his first trip to the Pro Bowl and a Second Team All-Pro selection. By 2012 the Seahawks had the fourth-

best defense in the league and an 11-5 record, led by First Team All-Pro Thomas.

Proving that defense wins championships, in 2013 the Seahawks won the franchise's first title in a 43–8 destruction of the Denver Broncos in Super Bowl XLVIII, with Thomas and the defense forcing four turnovers. Five-time NFL MVP Peyton Manning threw for only 280 yards and one touchdown on 49 attempts. Thomas had seven tackles, including one for a loss, and broke up a pass.

Thomas, along with Richard Sherman, has helped Seattle allow the fewest points in the NFL for three consecutive seasons, a feat not accomplished since the Minnesota Vikings did it from 1969 to 1971. And NFLsavant.com calculated that only 10 deep-middle passes were thrown in Thomas' area of coverage in 2014, which is just 1.87 percent of opponents' total passes. Of those, only four were completed.

Thomas made his fourth straight Pro Bowl and third consecutive First Team All-Pro in

2014, and the Seahawks made it back to the Super Bowl to defend their title. In the NFC Championship Game he separated his shoulder and was forced to miss just the second defensive series of his career. But he came back wearing a shoulder harness and was part of the Seahawks' miracle comeback and overtime win over the Green Bay Packers.

Facing the New England Patriots in the Super Bowl with a torn labrum, Thomas played all 74 defensive snaps and had nine tackles, as the team came within a few yards and one poor play call of back-to-back championships.

Thomas had surgery on his shoulder after the Super Bowl but will be back to start the 2015 season as the Seahawks try to reach their third straight title game. The man with the tattoo of a bloody football, who watched game film instead of a private Usher concert the night the Seahawks got their Super Bowl rings — and whom Sherman calls "The Example" — will be ready.

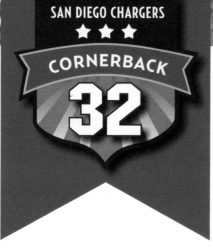

SAN DIEGO CHARGERS
CORNERBACK
32

ERIC WEDDLE

When asked what readers should take away from the book *No Excuses, No Regrets: The Eric Weddle Story*, the subject himself said, "A lot of people have told me what I can't do in this life, and that burned inside me every day. But I also surrounded myself with people who believed in me, supported and pushed me. Basically, what I'm saying is stay true to yourself . . . Don't ever let someone tell you that you can't do something. You define and decide your life and legacy, nobody else."

Born in Fontana, California, Weddle grew up in Alta Loma, east of Los Angeles, where he was twice named the Mt. Baldy League offensive *and* defensive MVP in high school. But he was only 5-foot-11 and 185 pounds — not your typical Division I prospect.

First recruited as a wide receiver in high school, Weddle shifted to quarterback as a senior, and major colleges lost interest. But Kyle Whittingham, the University of Utah's defensive coordinator at the time, wanted Weddle to come to his school as a defensive back. Whittingham's instincts were right. Upon arrival at Utah in 2003, Weddle was dominant. "He was by far the best at essentially every drill we did," Whittingham remembers.

In Weddle's junior year at Utah he was matched up against Calvin Johnson of Georgia Tech in the Emerald Bowl. Weddle made it a long day for the future NFL All-Pro, holding Johnson to two catches for 19 yards.

After that, Weddle says he believed for the first time that he could be an NFL player, and in his senior season in 2006 he proved it, earning distinction as the Mountain West Conference Defensive Player of the Year, as well as a First Team All-America selection.

In 2005, Weddle married Chanel, his high school sweetheart, who played soccer for rival Utah State. But April 28 2007, might be an even more important date. It's the day that the San Diego Chargers traded four picks to move up 25 spots and take the native of Southern California in the second round — 37th overall. It's also the day Chanel told him she was pregnant with their first child. The Weddles now have four children, and Eric has played eight seasons in San Diego.

It wasn't until his third year, 2010, that he became an All-Pro (Second Team) as San Diego led the NFL in passing defense after being second-last two seasons

earlier. Weddle hasn't missed a game since 2009, and he's been an All-Pro every year since 2010, getting his second First Team selection in 2014.

IN THE HUDDLE

As a senior at the University of Utah, Weddle became the first player in conference history to score touchdowns passing, rushing, on an interception return and on a fumble return in a season.

Weddle has amassed 772 career tackles and 19 interceptions, and his thick, lush beard has a Twitter account (@weddlesbeard),which he used to get the last word on former player and broadcaster Warren Sapp. In 2011, Sapp criticized Weddle's lucrative five-year contract, saying he couldn't pick the safety out of a lineup. After Sapp was arrested for solicitation the night of Super Bowl XLIX in early 2015, Weddle hit back with the hashtag #whoisinthelineupnow.

Even with the zingers, beard, awards and honors, Weddle has been called a "secret superstar" among safeties. It might have something to do with the small market in San Diego, or maybe it's because he's not on a Super Bowl winner, as is Seattle Seahawk Earl Thomas. At 5-foot-11 and only 200 pounds, he doesn't deliver the heavy highlight shots; he just patrols the middle of the field as a sure tackler and shutdown pass defender. He's become a field general and de facto assistant coach, while living a quiet family life off the field.

Purists recognize Weddle's oversized impact on games; pundits less so. After ESPN's Darren Woodson named his top-5 NFL safeties in 2013 and didn't include him, Weddle took

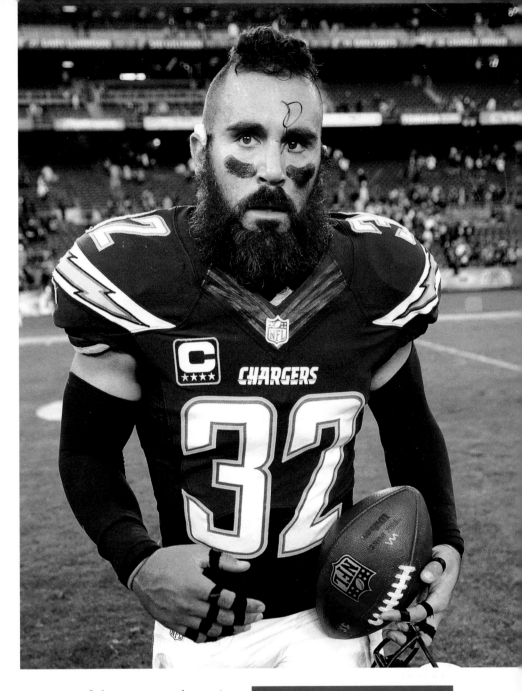

a picture of the screen and uses it for motivation.

"You can't honestly think there are four guys, five guys better than me in this league," says Weddle. "If you do, come down, let's watch everyone's film, and you show me. I honestly think if you put on film of me and everyone else in the whole game, your opinion of me would change dramatically."

Despite the doubters, those closest to Weddle recognize the legacy he's building.

"Where does he stack up?" asks John Pagano, the Chargers defensive coordinator. "He's the best."

CAREER HIGHLIGHTS

- Two-time First Team All-Pro selection (2011, 2014)
- Three-time Second Team All-Pro selection (2010, 2012–13)
- Three-time Pro Bowl selection (2011, 2013–14)
- Chargers' Most Valuable Player (2012)

Acknowledgments

Christine Moore,
for her love and patience

Steve Cameron, for also
providing the above

Jag Costescu, for paying
my Internet bill and being
the first in line to buy my books

Miguel Potenciano, for his
support — technical and moral

Frontier College, because
literacy is a right

And my family, always

PROFILE INDEX